There Was Once a Team

132-0 Winning Streak
5 State Championships

A memoir about the
Taylor County Lady Vikings of 1967-72

Cover Design: Gary G. Pulliam

ISBN: 978-1-935921-75-2
Library of Congress Number: 2021911612

This memoir is a true story, based on pictures, articles, and notes stored in scrapbooks the author made during the years the story takes place. Other source material includes news stories, the Lady Vikings Winning Streak blog, and student-produced movies. Any errors are not intentional.

Printed in the United States, Monroe, GA

Published by: BookEnds Publishing, Monroe, GA

Dedication

To Coach Norman Carter, who is the reason this story happened.

To the 1967-72 Taylor County Lady Vikings, who are still legends.

To Mark Harris and Ryan Dodrill, who helped to get this story told by being loving and supportive husbands.

To Sarah Grace Dodrill, who will one day read this story.

Table of Contents

Foreword

Although it has been a half century now, some old-timers in Taylor County swear they can close their eyes and still hear the bell ringing.

It's a memory, of course, sweeter than all the strawberry fields between Butler and Reynolds. Once upon a time, the bell hung from an oak tree next to Turk's Grocery. Folks rang it every time the Lady Vikings won a basketball game.

For five glorious winters, following games on Tuesday, Friday, and Saturday nights, it was like the sound of church bells on a Sunday morning.

The Taylor girls won a record 132 straight games and five state championships in three different classifications between 1967 and 1972, a stretch affectionately known as the "Wonder Years."

Those players and fans now look back with wonder. It was like shooting hoops every night for four and a half months and never finding yourself in the losing locker room. It remains the longest unbeaten streak in Georgia girls basketball history and the fourth-longest in the nation.

It began in the final game of the 1967 season, a meaningless win over Pike County in the consolation game of the region tournament. And it ended on January 4, 1972, in a packed gym in Perry, an upset so significant it was dispatched over the national wire services.

The string of victories was remarkable not only for its length but its depth. The streak had its roots in an era when the rules allowed only three players per side and then made the switch to "rover" six-player basketball in the 1970s. The Lady Vikings teams also won 63 consecutive games prior to integration, then helped smooth the transition of merging with the all-black R.L. McDougald High School by winning 69 more.

Norman Carter, the team's legendary coach, taught his girls to look him in the eyes when he spoke in the huddle and to use the back board on their jump shots. He taped their ankles tightly before every game and made sure they took their vitamins. He loved them like daughters.

Bunny Fuller Harris was one of his girls, and she became one of the program's all-time greats. She helped organize team reunions and become a proud historian of the Taylor basketball dynasty.

In her heart, she always knew this was a story that needed to be told.

Now it has been.

Ed Grisamore, Author and
Macon Telegraph columnist

There Was Once a Team

132-0 Winning Streak
5 State Championships

A memoir about the
Taylor County Lady Vikings of 1967-72

by

Bunny Fuller Harris
with Katie Harris Dodrill

Introduction

My scrapbook pages are disintegrating. The carefully clipped news articles have tape marks showing through, and the notes I wrote are getting faint. The corners that hold the pictures have long lost their glue. But even though my scrapbooks are fading, my memories are not.

Any story about the Taylor County Lady Vikings during the winning streak years begins and ends with our coach, Norman Carter. There is no other way to tell this story. He's the reason for the wins.

Over 700 teams played boys and girls high school basketball each year in Georgia during 1967-1972. But only one team won five state championships while winning 132 games in a row. Since that time, no team has matched that record of consecutive wins. The winning streak ranks number one in the history of basketball in Georgia and ranks fourth in the National Federation of State High Schools record book.

I was privileged to play on this famous team for four of the five championships and in 100 games of the 132 in the consecutive win record. I am proud to tell the story of our coach, our teams, our school and our community.

Taylor County faced many challenges from 1967-1972, making the years-long winning streak even more remarkable.

During the five seasons of the winning streak, there was complete turnover of players as some girls graduated and others took their places. Each year, the team had a different dynamic, a different atmosphere, a different flavor. As any coach knows, even if teams have many of the same players returning, no two teams or seasons are ever the same.

The rules of play changed during the course of the streak, going from the three-on-three rules to the rover rule, where two players could cross the center line and play offense and defense. Before this rule change, players were either forwards (playing only offense) or guards (playing only defense). With the rover rule, two girls on each team could become the "rover" who crossed the center line to the offensive or defensive end, making the end with the ball four-on-four.

Coach Carter changed roles at the school, moving from teaching to becoming high school principal in 1967 to being elected county school superintendent in 1968. In his various roles, he successfully led the schools and basketball teams through two of Taylor County's most tumultuous times: school consolidation and integration. The two county schools consolidated in the 1965-66 school year, a couple of years before the streak began, and then in 1970-71, right in the middle of the streak, the schools integrated. In the 1970-71 season, we meshed two schools and two teams (Taylor County High and McDougald High) and continued to win. Even after the biggest disappointment of our young lives when we finally lost a game in 1972, we picked ourselves up and won the state championship.

How did Coach Carter take teenage girls and mold them into unbelievable teams for five seasons in a row? He was a mastermind of the game, an awesome motivator, who learned from his teams in the past and devoted many hours of time to the teens of Taylor County.

The years of the winning streak were important and historic years for the Taylor County schools and community. With this memoir, I am preserving for future generations a story that shaped my life and those of my teammates, friends, coach, school, and county.

The Winning Streak Begins: 1967-68

Coach Carter, a native of adjoining Talbot County, came to Butler in 1960 with a degree from Mercer University to teach and coach basketball. Coach taught physics, chemistry, and history and coached all levels of boys and girls basketball while his wife Jane taught fourth grade in the Butler Elementary school. Their daughter Cathy was born in 1961 and their son Trey in 1966. I entered first grade at Reynolds Elementary in 1960, the same year that Coach came to Taylor County. My school career parallels Coach Carter's basketball career in that he coached twelve years and I was in the schools of Taylor County those same twelve years.

By the late 1960s, Coach Carter had learned a lot about coaching basketball and had been quite successful. He had coached both boys and girls basketball at Butler High School, and later Taylor County High School, for six of those years, winning the state championship in 1964 for Butler High with the girls and in 1966 for Taylor County High with the boys. Then came the 1966-67 school year, and the hopes of a state champion girls team were high.

The Lady Vikings were playing some good basketball in the winter of 1967 and came into the region basketball tournament in the Carroll County town of Bowden having won 22 in a row with an excellent chance at a region championship. The semi-final game of the region tournament, which determined whether the season continued, did not start well as one of our forwards broke her nose, but we were playing a good game and the score was close. Then, late in the game, senior Vicki Harris suffered a terrible ankle sprain that turned out to be a break (Coach Carter said her ankle "swole up like a balloon"). She tried to stay in the game with a tight taping of her ankle, but she just could not make it, and she couldn't finish the last game of her career. The momentum was lost as a Taylor County guard had to move to forward, and Westside of Rocky Face ended up beating the Lady Vikings by four points. Coach has said many times that had Vicki not broken her ankle, the number of consecutive state championships might have been six rather than five. The team was that good, and it's a shame their hopes were not fulfilled. A Macon Telegraph article by sports editor Harley Bowers quotes Coach Carter, "A week later a strong wind blew the top off the gym in Bowden, which I looked on as poetic justice for what happened to us there."

The region held a consolation game to determine third place. While that game may not have seemed too important at the time, it was the historic first game of the 1967-72 Lady Vikings winning streak — a win over Pike County on a cold and icy night in Bowden.

Sue Lawhorn, a junior member of the team, describes that night after the consolation win as one of tears and worry:

> "We had to spend that night at a motel because the icy roads were too dangerous to drive back to Butler. A rumor got started that Coach Carter was going to be principal at Taylor County High School the next year and that he was going to give up coaching. The story went that if he did coach, he would coach the boys. We girls all got so upset at the thought that we started crying. We were all crying so hard that we called Coach Carter to come to our room. We begged him to coach the girls the next year. We told him if he just would coach the girls, we would win every game for him. Did our crying spell convince him to coach the girls? I doubt it, but Coach Carter did decide to coach the girls, and we were all so glad. We won every game that next year."

The first full season of the winning streak began in the fall of 1967. Grace Bussey and Sue Lawhorn were standout seniors this year. Grace played guard, and her trademark was her one-armed throw to the forwards — she would reach her arm back and throw like a baseball player. Thinking back, I was surprised that Coach allowed that type of throw, but Grace was accurate, and Coach didn't change anything that worked for a player. He improved anything that didn't work and taught players his system. I always loved a picture that was captioned "Just Sissy and Sue" and showed Sue Lawhorn along with junior Sissy Riley - two great forwards. Sue was such a fun person; I knew before I met her that she was the life of the party. She came from a big family in Taylor County and was the jokester among the girls. She was quite an athlete and played the point guard position for the forwards with Sissy and Judy Riley on the wings. The team knew they could depend on Sue to keep the offense running.

During the 1967-68 season, the Lady Vikings had five matchups with Harris County. At one point in the season, the two teams played each other twice in seven days. Harris County did not lose to any team except Taylor County that year. If they hadn't played Taylor County, they would have had a perfect record. There were two meetings in the regular season, one home and one in Hamilton. The game at home in Butler was exciting, with Harris County leading by eight points at the half. Coach Carter describes a "soul talk" he gave the team at the half and said our team came up from the locker room in a better frame of mind. He said the team learned an important lesson that night: "The only person that can score is the one with the ball. We learned that we had to put pressure on the one with the ball all the time. We would not sit and watch a team pass the ball and dribble without action from our defense ever again." From that point on, he taught his teams to constantly pressure the one with the ball, cause turnovers, steal passes, rattle

Juniors Sissy Riley, Linda Joiner, and Diane Wall, back row, and seniors Grace Bussey and Sue Lawhorn, front row, with the four first-place trophies of the 1967-68 season.

My friend #25
had a Blast Linda Poole
#14

the opposing players, and most importantly, get the ball into the hands of our forwards more often. The result was more shots taken, more points scored, and more games won. The finals of sub-region and region saw Harris County play Taylor County. The resulting wins enabled the Lady Vikings to continue to state.

At state in 1968, the first game was against a Stone Mountain team who had lost their region final game, putting them in our bracket. Coach said he was worried because they were good, they were anxious for a win at the state tournament, and they had a woman coach. This game was the first time the Lady Vikings had played a team with a woman in charge. He was afraid we'd lose what we'd worked so hard for that year: a state championship. Coach joked that it would be bad enough to lose to a man, but to lose to a woman would be awful for him! The game turned out in our favor, with Sissy Riley having one of her best games, racking up eight points in a row early on and hitting at will the whole game. The first win of the 1968 state tournament was in the books 71-54. Coach didn't have to be embarrassed by losing to a woman, and he said when the woman coach shook his hand afterwards, she was still shaking her head as if she didn't know what hit her! The Lady Vikings soundly defeated Telfair County in the second round, setting up another matchup with Harris County.

Each time we faced Harris County, Taylor County was victorious. I'm sure Harris County fans were very hopeful that they'd pull an upset at the finals and finally defeat the girls from Butler in the Macon City Auditorium. In fact, the Macon Telegraph reporter described Harris County as starting the game without fear of falling again to Taylor County. But it was not to be anywhere near a win for them that night. Coach said senior Grace Bussey and juniors Diane Wall and Linda Joiner put on a defensive clinic in that game.

It was a defensive first half. Our guards held the Harris County Hornettes scoreless for seven minutes at one point. The score at halftime was a very low 17-10 with Taylor in the lead. Senior Sue Lawhorn, junior Sissy Riley and sophomore Judy Riley rounded out the Lady Vikings' team as the forward starters and the Harris County guards tried their best to rattle our scorers.

It was the last year the state tournament was played in the Macon

City Auditorium. All the players, from the boys state champion team of 1965-66 to the girls of 1967-68, say it was a wonderful place to play. The fans were close to the action in removable bleachers on the sidelines with the team. The auditorium seats in the balconies were full too. Cheers echoed off the domed ceiling. By the end of the night, there was a haze of smoke swirling in the ceiling. Playing in the Macon Auditorium had to have been a unique experience. Sissy Riley describes it:

> "I remember how Coach Carter covered every detail in preparing for games. Before we played in the state tournament in the Macon Auditorium, Coach had something unusual happen at practice. The Macon Auditorium had a balcony that was level with the glass backboards, so when you were shooting free throws, you could see all the fans waving and screaming at you to miss the shot. To get us used to this, he had several b-team boys climb up on the bars behind our backboards and sit there and wave and yell while we practiced shooting free throws."

During the third and fourth quarters of this final game against Harris County, the forwards Sue Lawhorn and Sissy and Judy Riley reeled off several strings of unanswered points. The lead expanded to 18 points twice, with the final margin 41-24. The hopes ended for Hornettes. For the fifth time that season, Taylor County High Lady Vikings defeated the Harris County team. Judy Riley wrote about Harris County, "Their star forward, Pat Robertson, wrote my sister Sissy a note congratulating us on our win. I think we must have earned that kind of respect by the way we played." Five players were named to the All-State Team: Sissy Riley, Linda Joiner, Diane Wall, Grace Bussey, and Sue Lawhorn. Sissy was named Most Valuable Forward in the state and Linda Joiner was named Most Valuable Guard in the state. The Lady Vikings left the Macon Auditorium that night with the State Class B State Championship trophy, a record of 31 and 0, a winning streak of 32 games, and a lot of respect.

Taylor County has two little towns: Butler (the county seat) and Reynolds about ten miles to the East, with other smaller communities spread through this geographically big county. I lived with my parents, Bernard and Lucibelle Fuller, in the Crowell Community. Crowell is in the panhandle of the county, nine miles from Reynolds and 11 miles from Butler. At the time I entered school in 1960, both of these little

No. 15 Sissy Riley drives for the basket with No. 25 Sue Lawhorn backing her up. No. 11 Diane Wall is waiting at the center line with the other guards.

towns had a first through twelfth grade school. There was both rivalry and respect between the Butler and Reynolds schools. Because Crowell Community was in the Reynolds district, I went to the Reynolds school when I started in 1960. The Butler and Reynolds high schools consolidated in 1965, when I was in sixth grade.

I got my first experiences playing basketball on the playground of Reynolds Elementary School. My class was taught each year by a different lady who was kin to someone in our class—cousins, aunts, grandmothers, and even our mothers. When my mother taught my class in fifth grade, she posted a bet with one of the little boys: "You'll catch up and pass Bunny in height by eighth grade." Alas, it didn't happen that soon, as I was always the tallest person in the class group pictures, often even taller than the teachers! I considered myself a giant, and was insecure, made more so by the mean boys who said, "How's the weather up there?" However, I quickly determined my height was an asset at recess when my prowess of shooting over everybody's arms made me many times the first chosen on the playground basketball teams, boy or girl. There were two basketball goals and one basketball for each class. Usually, a game would break out at the beginning of recess for our class of about 25 students. Back in those good old school days, we had a pretty long recess — long enough to choose teams and play a game, keeping score in the dirt with a stick.

My personal story of playing basketball includes my classmate Sandra Arnold in every sentence. We were not a lot alike. I was the tallest of the whole class, boys or girls, and she was among the shortest. She had sandy blonde hair and a permanent; I had bright red hair that was unruly and curly. She went home to a big family of five children. I was an only child. She wasn't much interested in grades. I, being a teacher's child, was very focused on grades. She lived in the midst of things, in town, among all the kids of Reynolds. I lived ten miles from town. Her dad was a bi-vocational preacher and her mom a nurse at the local hospital, and her dad was a Little League baseball coach and had been quite a baseball player himself. My parents and I were pretty much a party of three, staying in the country most of the time, with Daddy farming and working at various mechanic jobs, and Mama giving her all to me and to teaching school. Mama kept me busy with all kinds of lessons — from piano lessons begun when I was five, to Girl Scouts and 4-H. In other words, Sandra and I both had busy and different family lives, but we became so close on the basketball courts through the years that we could read each other's minds as we got older. We played basketball on teams together every year from seventh grade through twelfth grade. We each knew what the other was going to do on the basketball court before we did it.

During the 1967-68 school year, while the Taylor County Lady Vikings were beginning the famous winning streak, Sandra and I also played on an undefeated team at Reynolds Junior High. That was our eighth grade school year, and our coach, Mr. Harold Helms, scheduled games against any team from any big or small place within driving distance that would consent to play us. Mr. Helms accepted an invitation to go to Warner Robins, a big city close by, to play in a tournament with several of the junior highs over there, and the Warner Robins Sun newspaper had an article about the tournament. The first line reads, "Coaches at Tabor and Rumble Jr. Highs celebrated Easter early when they saw Bunnies in their sleep. The 'Bunny' was the eighth grade forward Bunny Fuller on the Reynolds team who scored 20 and 27 points to lead Reynolds Junior High to the championship."

Many years later, my brother-in-law Sandy Harris, who during these years was boys basketball coach at Taylor County High, told me that Coach Carter sent him to Reynolds soon after that tournament with these directions: "See if those girls are as good as I've heard, and find out if Mr. Helms is making a mess of their basketball knowledge." Sandy said he returned from our practice and told Coach, "Mr. Helms is not messing them up too badly, and they are some kinda good!"

Actually, Mr. Helms got his basketball knowledge from a booklet that he studied often and regularly read aloud to us at practice. I can still hear him in my mind, booklet in hand, reading to us in the old Reynolds gym. "There are three offensive maneuvers: pass the ball and cut away from the ball, pass the ball and cut toward the ball, or screen and then roll toward the goal." Then we'd practice each maneuver. The screen and roll became a most embarrassing moment for me in one of my first games. Alas, Mr. Helms had taught me to screen by completely blocking the opposing player with arms out wide and stiff to hold her from following the person she was guarding. I got called for two fouls for incorrect screening before the referee called a timeout to explain to Mr. Helms and me that I could not hold the player. He even demonstrated how a screen was supposed to be stationary with two feet on the floor. Oh, the embarrassment! However, Mr. Helms and our team worked hard, and we ended our eighth grade season 14-0.

In March 1968, Daddy and Mama took a couple of my friends and me to Macon to watch the Taylor County Lady Vikings play in the state championship at the Macon City Auditorium. It was amazing to watch them play with such precision and know that they'd won every game on their way to becoming state champions. As I watched the team surround Coach Carter afterwards, and several of the high school boys put him on their shoulders to ride him off the court after accepting the trophy, I was fascinated. I read every article in the Taylor County News about the team and followed every celebration they had after the win as community groups had banquets for them and churches invited the team to attend services. It started a dream in me to get on that team and play some basketball.

At the end of our eighth grade year, Coach Carter invited three Reynolds Tigers to come up to Butler to spring practice: Sandra and I, who were both forwards, and Jean Jones, who was a standout guard.

Taylor County's No. 13 Grace Bussey and No. 14 Linda Joiner play tenacious defense.

Being invited to practice with the Taylor County Lady Vikings was a big deal. Our mothers set about figuring out how we'd get to Butler for after school practice two days a week. I was taking voice lessons on Tuesdays in Butler, so our mothers decided that my mom would drive us all, I'd go take my lesson while Jean and Sandra went to the gym, and then I'd come to the practice late. I didn't like having to miss so much of the basketball practice, which was a lot more fun than voice lessons. But I figured I'd better just go along with the plan to get to go at all. I remember those few weeks very vividly. The Lady Vikings' practice was quite different from what I expected. When I arrived on the first day, Coach walked over, introduced himself, and said that I was to forget what I'd learned about shooting from Mr. Helms, which was a hook shot from the right side of the goal with my right hand and a hook shot from the left side of the goal with my left hand. I'd shot 50 hook shots a day in our practices in Reynolds and I was to forget I'd ever shot even one! Coach walked me over to a wall in the gym, handed me a ball, and commenced teaching me how to shoot a jump shot. At a wall, not even at a goal!

I didn't know it then, but a jump shot was one of the secrets to Norman Carter's success at coaching girls' basketball. Most girls don't naturally shoot a jump shot. While a very few natural athletes can do it, the majority of girls have to be taught how. Coach Carter believed every girl on his team who played forward could and would shoot a jump shot near the goal. He told us, "When you jump into the air, you go up awhile, then you pause and gravity makes you come down. For a jump shot, you release the ball when you're at the top of your jump, while you are hesitating in the air." It takes practice and strength, and he had us practice at the wall instead of the basketball goal until we got stronger. Coach Carter taught some girls to shoot two-handed. Sissy Riley was one of them. At the point she learned this skill, she was a little too weak to get the ball to the goal without using two hands, and her two-handed jump shot became her specialty. During those weeks of spring practice, I developed a right-handed jump shot. Eventually I got to move to the goal and learned the second step in Coach Carter's instruction: always use the backboard when you are close to the goal. "There is a square painted on there for a reason. Use it," he said. Aiming at the square made the shot more accurate, and I shot at that square from then on.

Learning about Coach Carter and his methods with the girls basketball teams was eye-opening for me. One incident that stuck with me was when Coach Carter was teaching us something and asked a question. We were scrimmaging and we had a jump ball tie up between two players. He explained how to line up around the circle for a jump ball. We were to hurry to the circle, pick the spot right in front of our team member jumping, and take up as much space as we could by having our feet at least shoulder length apart. "Why would you spread out like this?" Coach asked. I answered, "So you'll be ready to get the ball." I immediately noticed the collective shocked sigh from the other players, followed by silence. I was perceptive at least, and that reaction let me know that I'd done the wrong thing! You didn't answer Coach's questions. You waited for his answer and you ingrained that answer into your memory. From then on, I never said much of anything at practice, at games, in the hallways at school, anywhere I was around Coach. I bet I didn't say 50 words to Coach Carter that whole first year! I just listened and learned from Coach, and so did the rest of the team. From what I can remember, none of us talked that much to Coach. We certainly did not have the friendly, playful relationship that I saw some of his earlier teams have with him. He nicknamed me "Laryngitis" at one point because I said so little to him!

One night after I'd gotten home from a long day at eighth grade in Reynolds and then spring practice at the gym in Butler, I was out jumping on the trampoline when a car pulled up in the yard. Two tall men got out and one said, "Are you Bunny Fuller?" They said they were basketball coaches in Fort Valley and wanted to talk to my parents about my coming to Peach County for high school and playing basketball under them. In other words, they were coaches, and they were recruiting.

The reason Peach County coaches were recruiting a Taylor County student had to do with school consolidation. Reynolds and Butler High Schools had consolidated into Taylor County High School in 1965-66. I was mostly sheltered from the hard feelings in our county because my parents were supporting the consolidation, but I knew Reynolds didn't want to lose their high school. The people were proud of the record they had of smart students and good athletes (including an All-American, Ronnie Visage), and they wanted to continue sending their children right down the street to school, rather than 10 miles away from Reynolds to Butler. In anger and hurt, many families decided to send their children to Peach County. The spring of my eighth grade year, longtime friends in my class started announcing that they were not going to high school in Butler. We'd been together since first grade, so this split was very difficult for my class.

The two Peach County coaches went into the house and talked a short time with Mama and Daddy about how they'd heard about me from other students from Reynolds who attended high school in Peach County. They were nice and polite as Mama just listened to them. She really wasn't much interested in my playing basketball in high school. Basketball wasn't the most important thing to her, and she even asked them if I could play basketball as well as be in the band at their school. Taylor County High didn't have a band program at all. When they said that I couldn't do both, she was through with them, and after a polite listen to their spiel, she showed them out the door. A day or two later, those coaches mailed her an article about basketball and its good qualities for young folks. Somehow Coach Carter heard about the recruiting visit, and I always heard he got the coaches in trouble with the Georgia High School Association, using that mail-out as proof. Anyway, while it was flattering to have two coaches visit from a rival school, nothing would have changed my mind then about playing for the Taylor County Lady

Vikings, state champion team, undefeated in 31 games. No decision necessary. I had met Norman Carter and he had already worked his charisma on me in those few days of spring practice.

The rules of girls basketball at this time were called three-on-three basketball. Players were either forwards or guards. The role of forwards was to shoot the ball and score points on their end of the court. Forwards never crossed to the other end past center court. The guards kept the other team from scoring by playing defense, blocking out for the rebound when they shot, and returning the ball to the forwards at center court.

At that spring practice my eighth grade year, I met two girls who would become my adored lifelong friends. They were Sissy and Judy, known as the Riley sisters to anybody who mentioned Lady Vikings basketball. Those two were friendly, popular, and down-to-earth, and they were famous as two of the three starting forwards on the state championship team that year. Their house in the center of town was always hopping with teens playing ping pong under the carport. I wanted to be just like them, and that ambition has lasted my entire life.

The last day of spring practice, Coach Carter was working with me on pivoting to shoot the ball under the goal, and for some reason, he asked me what size my shoe was. I guess he had looked down at my feet and seen my embarrassingly huge Converse All-Star high tops. I answered as softly as I could, "Ten." He stopped his work with me, called for Sissy to come over from the other end of the court, and said, "Guess what size shoe Bunny Fuller wears? Size 10!" I could feel my face turn as red as my hair, but Sissy grinned to show that she was used to the ribbing and said, "Don't worry, I do, too!" Judy walked by about that time heading to the locker room and laughed at us both. Sissy said later in a description of our early friendship, "I was glad for Bunny to join the team for lots of reasons, most especially to have someone else share my shoe size. I always said that it took a lot to knock us over!" The four forwards (Sissy, Judy, Sandra, and me) spent a lot of time together, and Sandra joked, "You all were so tall I had to trot to keep up with you!" I think it was Judy who gave the nickname "Shrimp" to Sandra, and it's stuck with her to this day.

Winning a state championship in a small town is definitely a source of great pride for the whole area. By the time I attended spring practice, Coach Carter had won three state championships and become a town hero. On Saturday of the last week of spring practice, there was a huge hoopla honoring Coach Carter, called Norman Carter Day, for the recognition he'd brought to the county through his basketball program. It was organized by Buddy Dunn, a member of the local Jaycees, and included a parade in Coach's honor with floats from almost every club and organization in the county. I helped with the Crowell Community 4-H Club float and rode on it during the parade. Mama and Daddy and I attended the recognition program in the high school gym that night, and it made a distinct impression on me. I watched Coach Carter closely, and he seemed so uncomfortable and appeared to wish he could hide under the chair as he sat there with his beautiful wife Mrs. Jane. However, Taylor County had learned to love him as coach, teacher, and principal, and he had to accept the accolades of the parade and the program. As I listened to the program, I could not wait to begin my ninth grade year at Taylor County High and my basketball career with the Lady Vikings.

Jane Carter, Coach Norman Carter, Norman Carter, Sr. and Mary Virginia Carter at the parade held in Coach's honor.

Sissy Riley and Sue Lawhorn during the 1967-68 season.

The gym was built in 1953 and is still in use for practice and P.E. courses. The Lady Vikings never lost a game in the years 1967-72 in this gym.

Winning Streak Season 2: 1968-69

Coach Carter continued as principal of the high school in Fall 1968. He was elected Taylor County School Superintendent in August and would take office in January of 1969. He had already asked the school board if he could continue coaching the girls basketball team, saying, "The girls have that winning streak going, and I need to coach them at least as long as they are winning." They agreed, not knowing that the winning streak would continue for nearly four more years.

Basketball practice began. With three-on-three basketball, there are three forwards and three guards (six on the court for each team), but the forwards and guards are never together on the same end. Only one starting forward, Sue Lawhorn, had graduated. The Riley sisters were returning, Sissy a senior and Judy a junior, and they were champions. Sissy had been named Most Valuable Forward in the state during the 1967-68 season. Judy had started in all 31 undefeated games, and was versatile in that she was good under the goal at rebounding and putting the ball back in the goal, had a good set shot from the top of the key, and also was an excellent passer. Of course, the Riley sisters were starters on this 1968-69 version of the Lady Vikings. That left one position open on the forward end, and Sandra Arnold and I had established ourselves at spring practice as vying for that position. At practices, we got plenty of work on both individual skills and teamwork. During scrimmages, sometimes Coach would play Sissy on the left side, Judy on the right side, with Sandra as point guard, and other times it would be Judy as point guard, with Sissy on the left side, and me on the right side. Who would get the starting job with the Riley sisters? I don't remember dwelling on it much, because I was just adjusting to high school, which seemed huge after attending the little Reynolds school, and I was loving practice, becoming friends with all those great girls and learning so much about every facet of the game from Coach Carter. Being welcomed onto that team was wonderful. There were standouts like Linda Joiner, Diane Wall, Sissy and Judy Riley, Denease McAbee, Patsy Ranow, and twin guards Kathy and Karon Peed. I could tell these girls absolutely loved being a part of the team.

No.15 Sissy Riley and her sister No. 34 Judy Riley at the State Tournament in Macon Coliseum with No. 11 Diane Wall and No. 14 Linda Joiner in the background.

One day at practice, Coach announced that he and Mrs. Jane were having a cook-out for the team at his house in a couple of days. We gathered at the Carters' house on Highway 19 north of Butler, and Mrs. Jane served hotdogs with all the trimmings. Then we all played the silliest games in the front yard of Coach's house, like Hide and Go Seek and Red Light. I learned that these champion basketball players didn't have a stuck up or mean bone in their bodies, and they welcomed even the lowly freshmen onto the team. I particularly remember seniors Linda Joiner and Diane Wall, two guards, being the friendliest and most welcoming of the whole bunch. Linda was boisterous and fun, getting us organized for the games and silliness, while Diane was quiet and unassuming, but smiling the whole time. It was great to be a Lady Viking!

The first game of the year in the 1968-69 season was late October, right around Halloween. About two weeks before, we'd gotten our uniforms and our schedule cards, little business cards with the entire schedule of 20 home and away games printed on them along with advertisements from local businesses. Excitement for the season was mounting. Sissy said, "We were lucky that there were not a lot of other distractions in town because everyone was concentrating on basketball. We didn't realize how great we had it, we just knew it was fun." Taylor County High School did not have a football team at that time, so basketball was the main sport, and it seemed that everyone in town came to the games.

Coach Carter called us four forwards together on one end of the court one day and announced that we would alternate the starting line-up at forward game by game. It would work like this. When it was my turn, I would be the starter the first quarter with Sissy and Judy, Sandra would play the next quarter with Sissy and Judy, and Sandra and I would play the third quarter with Sissy. Coach Carter would decide who'd play in the fourth quarter during each game. The next game, Sandra would be the starter, and we'd rotate quarters in the same way. Sandra and I would both be considered as "first string" forwards on the Lady Vikings. Because of Coach Carter's decision, the jealousy which could have inevitably crept between Sandra and me didn't have a chance to start. We didn't have to compete with each other but instead could concentrate on competing against the opposing team.

Finally, the season arrived, and we played our rival Crawford County for the first game of the 1968-69 year. Being adjoining counties always made this a game with a huge crowd, and to this freshman's eyes the experience was both terrifying and exciting. The coach of Crawford County for the boys and the girls was the unforgettable J. B. Hawkins. I'd heard the story about the first year of Coach's career: how J. B. Hawkins had taken one look at young Coach Carter carrying the mesh bag of basketballs and said loudly to one of our players, "You can tell the ball boy to put the basketballs over here beside the score table." Of course, Coach Hawkins knew exactly who Coach Carter was. He was just giving the new kid on the block trouble, but he soon probably wished he hadn't after Coach's teams started dominating the Taylor vs Crawford games. We won that first game of the season 72-32, and my first season as a Lady Viking was off to a great start.

Once the season began, our practices changed to include intense preparation for the next team we would play. Coach Carter's description of the upcoming team might include, first to the starting guards, "This player will only drive to the right. She's right-handed and won't even look to her left. They are strong rebounders so we've got to block them out. They screen players a lot to get their players a shot, so be sure to yell, 'Screen, get through' or 'Screen, switch' where the whole gym can hear you." The forwards heard something like, "Their defense will be double-teaming Sissy, so somebody else will be open until they learn that all of you can shoot." Coach always made us feel confident in our shooting ability. "Judy or Bunny, go to the goal when you see your guard leaving. Sandra will get the ball to you. Judy or Sandra, watch for an open shot from the top of the key as they drop back on Sissy." Our b-team players, or "Rinky Dinks," gave the team a chance to practice each situation Coach Carter described and were very important to the team. Coach Carter never practiced the starting guards against the starting forwards, reasoning that team members should save their best efforts for the games. He said our Rinky Dinks were really good, better than other teams' starters, and that they'd get the job done at practices. And they did. My good friend Jean Jones said, "I was still a freshman when senior Maxine Lawhorn explained to me that I was a Rinky Dink. Ordinary teams had benchwarmers, but even the Lady Vikings' bench was a step above other teams' benches and had its own proud name. Maxine may have been joking, but that's sure what we called ourselves — the Rinky Dinks. It was part of the tradition of Lady Viking basketball."

One important element of getting ready for each game was the ankle taping; rather than giving the job to a manager, Coach personally taped ankles. After Vicki Harris's ankle injury cost an important win in 1967, he said if he could help it, he wouldn't lose another game because of a sprained or broken ankle. Before the game, he'd tape our ankles so tightly that we could barely bend them to walk. The tape would loosen during the game, but in the locker room after the games it was a pain to get the tape off our socks. The managers were assigned to help, and I'm sure that task was unpleasant, but our managers, led by Joyce Kendrick and Melodie Bohler, did whatever was asked of them. They made a game to see who could remove the tape the fastest.

Practices had a focused and solemn feel throughout the year. From the time we stepped on court in our shorts, t-shirts, and white canvas Converse All-Stars, we were learning and doing. Since Coach

Carter was principal, we could count on his knowing what was going on in the school classrooms as well as around town. Sandra remembers, "Once he lined us up against the wall after practice and said someone had failed an algebra test. He wouldn't name the person but said, 'You know who you are.' He said he had talked to the teacher and this person would be allowed to take the test again the next day and 'You had better pass.' Of course I went home and studied my butt off and made a 94 on the test. I was so nervous because I knew if I failed again Coach Carter could remove me from the team. Basketball was my life so I never failed another test. (Thanks Mr. Dwight!)" Mr. Dwight Harris was our county math whiz who taught almost everyone on the team, and we were all a little worried Coach was referring to us as the person who failed.

We weren't threatened by any team this season, with margins of victory in the teens for most games. The forwards, Sissy, Judy, Sandra, and I were thriving. We scored plenty of points every game because the guards were doing their job of getting the ball to us on our end of the court for score after score. Sissy was awesome, scoring over 50 points some games even though she unselfishly would pass off the ball many times when she saw one of us with a more open shot. She was double-teamed more times than not, which left one of us open to score easily. The opposing team would try other strategies, but nothing worked to stop Sissy. She was our ace!

Coach Carter always said that guards had to be smart. He said he could teach a monkey to shoot, but guards had to have finesse and a head on their shoulders. I had great respect for the guards and loved to watch them during the games. The year before, Linda Joiner had been named Most Valuable Guard in the state and Diane Wall had been named an All-State player. Both seniors lived up to their awards. They were tenacious defensive players and competitive, but just as nice as could be. When they took the court, it was with an air of leadership, and they started every game. The guards were loaded with talent that year, with juniors Denease McAbee and Peed twins Kathy and Karon, as well as sophomore Patsy Ranow. Coach said that these girls played defense so well he honestly couldn't choose among the four underclassmen, so he just alternated starters.

After school before many of the away games, Sandra and I went to Sissy and Judy's house, and the six starting guards went to

Coach Norman Carter instructs the guards on defensive strategy. L to R: Patsy Ranow, Linda Joiner, Denease McAbee, Diane Wall, Kathy Peed, Karon Peed, Coach Carter.

Coach Carter's home. I don't remember how this habit started, but it did ensure that those of us who lived in other areas of the county would be at the school when the bus was ready to pull out for the away game. Spending so much time together also led us to become closer friends and teammates. While we had a lot of fun together, Coach said we were expected to rest some during the afternoon. Providing supper for us before the game while also taking care of their own families and getting ready to head to the game themselves certainly caused extra work for Mrs. Jane and Mrs. Sarah (Sissy and Judy's mom), but they always seemed to enjoy it. It seemed Mrs. Sarah was always driving us one place or another, chaperoning when we went on overnight trips, and generally looking after us. She helped sew our travel outfits, and when I got blisters on my feet, she advised me to wear two pairs of socks. Her husband Mr. Frank was always ready with a story or some sage advice, and we knew we could count on them for anything we needed. After many of our home games, Mr. Frank, Mrs. Sarah, Mama, Daddy, me, the Riley girls, and other fans would stand around on the court and talk awhile. I will always treasure those memories.

The gym at Taylor County High had been built in 1953 by J. E. Bone as a gymnatorium, which meant it doubled as an auditorium for the school. To my eyes, it was beautiful. When fans walked up those steps into the arched entryway and bought their tickets at the small admissions window, they immediately saw the basketball court. The floors gleamed, and the mounted electric fans high up on the gym ceiling loudly stirred up a breeze in the humid Georgia air. In the winter, big mounted heaters blew warm air. Fans reached the bleachers by climbing up steep stairs on either far end of the court. Wood bleachers started about head height on one side, and on the opposite side, temporary bleachers were set up on the stage, making the gym hold about a thousand people. Dungeon-like basement locker rooms were below the stage for home teams and visitors. The players sat in chairs at court level, both teams on the right side of the court. The home team met in the basement behind those chairs, and the visitors met in the locker room. The scoreboard on one end had an analog clock that ticked down the minutes and seconds until a loud squawk signaled announcements of end of quarter, substitution of players, and end of game. The fan-shaped fiberglass backboards towered above the court from long metal beams.

There are so many memories from that old gym in Butler. I remember the exact spot my parents sat. Looking back, I wonder if I ever told them enough that I appreciated them coming to every game. Both would be tired from a full day of working - Mama teaching elementary school and Daddy driving the Gulf Oil gas truck. They'd get home, eat a quick supper, and Daddy would have to feed up the livestock before we headed to the game. After getting me to the gym early, they'd settle in their favorite spot and wait for the game to start. The gym included a stage since it doubled as an auditorium, and on the stage side there was very little room between the basketball court and the bottom of the elevated stage. A single row of chairs could fit there for a row of fans, and that's where a lot of the parents chose to sit. Mama and Daddy sat there every home game because it was more comfortable to sit in a chair than on the backless bleachers. Daddy would enjoy the games immensely, and especially liked watching the boys' coach Sandy Harris (my future brother-in-law). Sandy was a fiery and emotional coach, very exciting to watch. He would sometimes get mad at the referees and many times by night's end, he would have kicked the chair against the wall until it folded up and crashed against the gym floor. Daddy particularly loved that move, and he'd laugh and talk about it when we got home. Mama was a different story. She'd loyally support the teams, but she never could follow the game. She'd often be daydreaming about other things during the game, and I'd see her lost in thought when I glanced her way. I'd tease her mercilessly, asking, "Mama, can't you at least watch the end of the court where the action is, even if you don't know what's going on?" We joked about her not paying attention to the game my entire basketball career.

Basketball teams also include many additional positions such as the managers/statisticians and the cheerleaders. This year, managers Joyce Kendrick and Melodie Bohler were assigned a room in the gym for their equipment, and Joyce made a sign for the door labeled "Manger Room." Coach Carter has never let her forget that spelling mistake! As Melodie Bohler illustrates, the managers had the same respect bordering on fear of Coach Carter as the players did:

> "One of my biggest tests came very soon after I was 'hired.' At that time, Coach Carter drove a light blue Ford Falcon. It had a manual transmission with the stick on the steering column. When Coach Carter asked me if I could drive a straight shift, I told him I could. But I really couldn't. I was afraid I'd get fired, so I quickly got a friend to show me how to change the gears in her father's pick-up truck. Soon, one afternoon, Coach Carter asked me to drive to the drugstore and get vitamins for the players. Changing the gears wasn't the hard part. The hard part was synchronizing the clutch with the gas. This skill comes with experience, of which I had very little. To begin with, the car choked down a lot when starting and stopping. I learned to 'pop' the clutch, which worked, but did not provide a very smooth ride. Needless to say, Joyce and I had some memorable trips to town."

The cheerleaders were another big part of the basketball teams' success, supporting us throughout the games with great cheer routines. Mrs. Jeri Harris, the cheerleading sponsor (who later became my sister-in-law), was the envy of many of us girls at Taylor County High School.

She had recently married boys coach Sandy Harris, and they were a popular couple at the school. Jeri was so stylish in her Villager skirts and tops, with Pappagallo shoes and John Romaine pocketbook. Her hair was always in the latest style, a short bob with bangs. She was petite, but packed a huge punch in her French and English classrooms. Making the cheerleading squad was a highly competitive affair that girls aimed at for years. A favorite cheer that year came from the expression "Sock it to me!": "Sock it to the East, Sock it to the West, When you sock it to the Vikings, you've socked it to the best!"

A few weeks into the new year of 1969, we headed to Manchester for the games of the Tri-County Invitational Tournament, a storied tournament said to be the "oldest invitational basketball tournament in Georgia." I liked the Manchester gym, mainly because it had these old-fashioned fan-shaped metal basketball goals that I shot well at. They reminded me of the old Reynolds goals from my junior high years. My first game during the tournament was memorable to me because I scored the first eight points of the game. Sissy was double-teamed with my guard leaving me. Coach had taught us well. When your guard leaves you, go to the goal. Judy just passed it to me and I scored — easy peasy! When the other coach called timeout to make some changes in his game plan, I remember looking at the scoreboard and giggling as I realized I'd scored all of the eight points we had at that point. That timeout put an end to my easy scoring, though. Next time we got the ball, I had a guard on me. Most invitational tournaments were held during Christmas vacation, but this one took place over the course of two weekends, with the first games on a Friday and Saturday and then the semis and finals on the following weekend. Many years we had a game on Tuesday night between the two weekends of the Tri-County tournament.

On Saturday night, after the quarter-final game in Manchester, we went to visit Coach Carter's father. It was so much fun to meet an older version of our coach, his dad Mr. Norman King Carter, Sr. He and his wife made us feel so important and special. I particularly remember that there was a Hammond organ in the living room and he sat down to play it a little. He talked and joked with us, very different from Coach's relationship with us. It was just a fun end to a very fun night — winning the early round of the Tri-County Tournament and preparing to return the next weekend.

The most memorable game to everybody at that tournament was the Greenville game we played in the finals. Greenville gave us a run for our money, and they were leading the game by seven points at the end of the third quarter. We were well on our way to getting beaten and losing our streak. The Manchester paper describes the second half: “The fabulous Sissy Riley put on a scoring exhibition.” Coach Carter said later, “The guards won that game with their excellent defense in the third and final quarters.” However, being a forward, I felt we won because Sissy ended up with 42 points. Either way, game number 51 of the streak was in the books. Sissy and Judy Riley both made the All-Tourney team as well as Linda Joiner and Dianne Wall. We were Tri-County Champs for the Lady Vikings’ second year in a row.

In January of 1969, Coach moved from high school principal to school superintendent and had many pulls on his time. He would come in to practice, sometimes in coat and tie straight from a meeting, and he’d have a tiny piece of an envelope with the day’s practice schedule in his shirt pocket. Once, I saw the schedule, and I was amazed at how detailed it was, with exact times like “3:12 - 3:19 Forwards shooting, Guards work against screens, 3:20 - 3:25 Jump ball strategies, 3:26 - 3:35 Forwards out of bounds plays, guards half-court press.” Every minute of every practice was planned. The only minutes left to chance were at the end of practice. A lot of days Coach would have the forwards shoot free throws as a pair, saying, “Six in a row before you can go.” Our teams of two had to shoot two, swap, shoot two, swap, until as a team we had rung six baskets in a row. Two of us would be on one end of the court and the other two forwards would be on the other end. I always felt the pressure when my team would get to five and it was my turn to shoot and determine if we went home or started over. We’d get six in a row eventually, and it was a confidence builder when our team of two did it. This exercise also was the greatest way to learn to shoot free throws in games. Just like in a real game, we were tired when we started, we only shot two at a time, and we were under pressure to make the shots. The exercise also emphasized the importance of teamwork as we worked to get six in a row.

Details were important to Coach Carter, and he had us prepared for every situation. Our next opponent, Pike County, had a team known for their defense, and their guards were ferocious.

Coach had the Rinky Dinks simulate their questionable tactics during practice before the sub-region tournament. "Push, shove, hold them, even pinch and poke the sides of our forwards as they stand at the center line," he'd tell the Rinky Dinks. Practicing these extreme tactics did prepare us for the game against Pike County. Jim Cosey describes the game in his column in the Taylor County News: "I noted a few instances of 'weird' guarding in the game. Pike County would completely envelope Sissy at the center line. While she was waiting for the guards to get the ball down to center court, the Pike County guards would stand around Sissy, holding hands. I'm not sure whether this is legal or not, but it was not called a violation, so I guess it is. But, I think that's pretty dirty." This game was in the semi-finals of the sub-region, an all important game that determined if the team got a berth in the state tournament. The Pike County Pirates held the lead most of the game, but we came back in the fourth quarter to win it by 14 points behind the scoring of Sissy and Sandra with 26 and 16 respectively. I remember Pike County as being a worthy opponent. I'm glad we won that all-important game and beat Milner the next night for the region championship.

The games of the first round of the 1969 State Tournament were held at various locations around the state. Coach Carter, being superintendent as well as coach, was a very busy man. Our first game was held in Talbotton at the Talbot County High School gym against Toombs Central. We were right in the middle of the second quarter of a pretty tight game when the most unusual thing happened. A little man came running over to the Taylor County bench with a worried look on his face, got right in front of Coach where he couldn't even see the game, and as Coach motioned for him to move, he said, "Are you Norman Carter? You have an emergency phone call in the office." Long distance calls were pretty rare in 1969, and hearing the word "emergency" had to have been scary for Coach. He called time-out and asked the nearest official if he could leave the court to take an emergency phone call, and then hurried to the office in the gym. When he answered the phone, he heard the principal of Reynolds Elementary, "This is Harold Helms. Mr. Carter, what temperature do you want the thermostat on tonight at the elementary school - 68 or 72?"

I'm sure Coach's blood pressure went pretty high that game,

and not just because of the "emergency." Toombs gave us a good game, leading at halftime. After a rousing locker room talk from Coach, we picked up our play. The Macon Telegraph article says, "Fuller got a hot hand and scored ten points in the third quarter." We took the lead then and maintained it to win 46-25. We'd be heading to Macon for the rest of the tournament. We had the first game out of the way and were hoping for three more on the way to winning the State Championship.

The Georgia High School Association had decided to move the 1969 State Basketball Championship from the Macon City Auditorium to the new Macon Coliseum. We'd never been inside, so earlier in the season, Coach Carter took the team over to see a Hawks exhibition game and get a feel for the place. We walked in the front door and saw this huge expanse of seats on all sides, with the basketball floor far below. The wall that divides the lobby from the open Coliseum was not there as it is now, and the view was unobstructed from the lobby to the seats on the other end of the court. It was an awesome sight, the biggest place this 15 year old country girl had ever seen. I well remember the nervous, excited feeling in the pit of my stomach when I thought of playing basketball before a crowd in that huge place. Coach saw our expressions and laughingly said, "Before I played games, I would have hummingbirds instead of butterflies, but when the ball went up for the center jump they all flew away."

Our first game in the Macon Coliseum was on March 20th, 1969, and was the quarter final round. We had played the first round on March 15th, so we had nearly a week to get ready, and the media had that week to tout the upcoming game as a "Dream Match." Our opponent was Doerun, the defending state Class C champions. The Lady Vikings were the defending state Class B champions. Everyone expected a close game.

The basketball court at the Macon Coliseum was removable, and the joke among the players was that if we could all just run out on the court to warm up without tripping over the raised edge, everything would be all right. The ball bounced on the court with a hollow sound, and the voices of our guards hollering "Screen, get through," were drowned in the cavernous building. The goals had clear backboards, and getting our depth perception against that expanse of space between goal post and bleachers was difficult. But I'd say the Lady Vikings overcame those obstacles fairly well.

The "Dream Match" against Doerun quickly became a nightmare — but not for us! Our guards held their forwards to only three points in the whole first quarter, while our forwards scored 19 points. Senior Sissy Riley scored 35 points that night. Although Doerun kept trying to catch up, that early lead was too big, and we ended up winning that first game in the Macon Coliseum 63-39. In Jim Cosey's editorial column, Mrs. Sarah Riley calls the Coliseum, "a nice place to have a nervous breakdown." Judy said later that her mother lost weight during basketball season from being so worried. After that first game, though, the Lady Vikings decided we loved the Coliseum.

During the state tournament, an article came out in the Macon Telegraph about Sissy Riley titled, "Taylor County's Supergirl is a Sissy!" It was written by John Krueger, the Assistant Sports Editor, and it begins, "She doesn't change into her uniform in a telephone booth, but that, along with the fact that she looks a heckuva lot better, are about the only differences between Clark Kent and Taylor County's 'Basketball

No. 15 Sissy Riley shoots her patented two-handed jump shot in the finals of state vs. Cave Spring. Sandra Arnold heads in for backup with guards Patsy Ranow, Linda Joiner, and Denease McAbee waiting at the center line.

Supergirl' Sissy Riley. In keeping with the Superman image, 'Sissy' isn't her real name. It's Elizabeth." The article goes on to describe Sissy as one of the finest girls basketball players in the state, past or present, labeling her as the offensive key to Taylor County's 63 straight victories and two consecutive state championships. Coach Carter is quoted, "The amazing thing is Sissy has rarely played an entire game because only if the game is close or if we're behind do we leave her in. One night, we were involved in a close game and she played the entire 28 minutes. She scored 53 points." Sissy says of the pressure caused by the winning streak, "It mounts with each game. We try not to think about it during a game, but sometimes it's hard, especially if we're losing." Sissy's uniform, number 15, was retired at the end of the season, and there would never be another as great as Sissy Riley in all the years of the streak.

After that first tournament game, we spent the night in Macon at the Alpine Lodge. We had fun, but the girls in one room got in trouble. After the time for lights out, Linda Joiner and three other girls were using flashlights to play Password when they heard a rap at the door and Coach Carter called Linda's name. Linda said her heart dropped to her toes. What had happened to the lookout managers who were supposed to warn them with a cough if Coach came by? Linda said Coach called her name twice more before she was able to answer.

"Coach said, 'Didn't I tell you what time to have lights out and go to sleep? Well, I meant it!' 'Yes, sir,' I said, and we went to sleep. The next morning we four were all so scared. We just knew we'd be benched and wouldn't be playing that night at all. The other players avoided us at breakfast and all morning. They didn't want to get in trouble with us. Finally Coach came to our room and told us that we weren't going to be benched, that he just wanted us to get our rest before the big game. We all breathed a sigh of relief."

In one of our practices before the tournament, Coach taught us a play he called the freeze. He set up the scoreboard with us ahead by three points with only a few seconds, and said that in this situation in a game, he'd signal the guards to freeze in their positions. By that he meant just what he said — freeze with no movement at all. Freezing would allow the other team to drive straight into the goal for a layup. They might score two points, but that would not be enough to win or tie the game.This tactic looked funny on the court, especially to the opposing fans, but it definitely worked, as we found out soon in our game against Cave Spring.

Taylor County won the semi-final game against Glascock County easily and headed to the final game against Cave Spring. It was a low scoring battle between two great coaches and defenses. Cave Spring was picked to beat us. Many people came early to see the Cave Spring Springers warm up. Most of their girls had their hair in cute little pigtails with ribbons, and they ran out with jump ropes in their hands. For the first few minutes, instead of practicing their shooting and getting used to the goals, they did fancy jump rope routines! Their coach was quite a bit older than ours, and he was certainly old school in his approach to basketball. His game plan was one we'd seen teams try before but not successfully: the stall offense. The idea was if the Lady Vikings couldn't get the ball, we couldn't score. Each time the forwards from Cave Spring got the ball, they'd slow it down, hold the ball for a few seconds, dribble in and out from the hash mark to center court, and never go toward the goal to set up their offense until their coach's signal. The point of this maneuver was to run minutes off the clock with neither team scoring. Of course, we were drilled in what to do when a team tried a stall offense against us. Our guards pressed them the whole game. Whenever a girl had the ball, our guard stayed close to her, making her go the direction she didn't want to. If she was right handed, our guards made her dribble left. Then when she stopped dribbling our guard was all over her, trying to keep her from passing the ball successfully. The other guards were covering the passing lane between her and her other forwards. The opposing players had been coached not to go toward the goal, so of course we'd practiced making them go toward the goal. Their team was good, well-coached, and obviously following their game plan. It is really hard to maintain a stall offense for very long, and they did it pretty well. An amazing statistic to me was that we were held to only two points the whole second quarter. That's because we forwards didn't get the ball.

The score was tied 13-13 at the half, a ridiculously low score. The third quarter resumed with more of the same. At one point, Coach Woodell got frustrated with his team, and Coach Carter swears that he saw Coach Woodell with a girl over his knee paddling her! Many years later, in describing that scene, Coach said, "What would Frank and Sarah Riley have done to me if I'd paddled Sissy or Judy like that?!"

With 45 seconds left in the game, we had the ball on the forward end and Coach called time out. He knew they were expecting us to work the ball to Sissy Riley for the last shot, but instead, he set up a play involving freshman Sandra Arnold. Sissy was to make a cut like she was expecting the ball and move over to the same side of the lane as me, making a clear-out for Sandra to drive the lane. It was executed perfectly. Sandra faked a pass to Sissy as she cut across the lane. The guard left her feet to try to deflect the pass. Sandra then made a giant first step around her with a couple of dribbles and laid the ball off the backboard into the goal. We were ahead by six points. Cave Spring called a time out with 20 seconds left. During the timeout, Coach instructed our three guards Denease McAbee, Diane Wall, and Linda Joiner to go to their position on the court and stand there with their hands by their sides. "Do not move," he said. "They can't score enough to beat us now." We were using the freeze technique that we had practiced, and it worked perfectly. It looked kind of comical with our guards standing in the lane, not making a move at all, just watching the other team handle the ball. The Cave Spring forwards were so amazed that no one was guarding them that they almost dropped the ball, but they recovered and drove right through our guards for a lay-up without a movement from Taylor County. However, two points was not enough to catch us. We got the ball then at center court and held it as the clock ticked down to zero. Two state championships in a row for the Lady Vikings! We won by a score of 36-32 in the lowest scoring contest of the winning streak years for the Lady Vikings.

Coach Carter had promised that if we won the State Championship, he'd jump in the motel pool after the game on that cold March night. A large crowd of supporters followed us back to the Alpine Lodge to watch. Coach Carter jumped in, followed by several players. Denease McAbee, Linda Joiner, and Sissy Riley all ended up in the pool, either jumping or being pushed in during the boisterous celebration. What a night for the Lady Vikings! We'd won the state championship and kept our winning streak alive with 63 straight wins.

One of the best parts about our winning streak was our fans. At that time, people would dress up in their best clothes (men in suits and ties, women in dresses) to attend games. After the state tournament, local families and businesses would host banquets for the team at restaurants. A girls team getting so much attention was fairly unusual at that time. Newspapers would often dismiss the girls games as the preliminary before the boys games, but the Lady Vikings changed that idea. We put on a show that people loved to watch. With the ending of this season, games 33-63 of the winning streak were in the history books. Little did we know the streak would continue to more than double this number of wins.

No. 14 Linda Joiner, No. 11 Diane Wall, and No. 44 Denease McAbee play defense at the state tournament. Forward No. 15 Sissy Riley waits on the opposite end of the court.

Lady Vikings waiting for State Championship trophy presentation. L to R: Sissy Riley, Diane Wall, Beth Barrow, Judy Riley, Regina Parks, Sandra Arnold, Patsy Ranow, Denease McAbee, Karon Peed, Linda Joiner, Maxine Lawhorn, Bunny Fuller, Dianne Kendrick

Winning Streak Season 3: 1969-70

One day during the summer of 1969, Daddy came in from the mailbox across the road from our house in Crowell Community and said, "Bunny, you've got a postcard." It was addressed to Bunny Fuller, Reynolds, GA. The letter had no zip code, address line, or return address, but it got to me with no problem. In Taylor County, everybody knew everybody! There was one sentence on the other side: "Report to school in good condition, both mentally and physically. Coach."

Looking back now, the 1969-70 version of the Lady Vikings was probably my favorite year. We were a well-oiled machine on offense, and on defense we were loaded with talent. I was really looking forward to the season starting in November.

Before the season, the seniors decided on the "away" outfits for the year, the outfits we would wear while traveling to other schools. They chose a McCall's pattern and asked several ladies to sew the herringbone fabric into cute double-breasted jumpers. We had several mothers who took on the sewing task, and the seniors measured us all for our jumpers. Dianne Kendrick, who was a junior this year, said she always felt that we made quite an impression on other teams and their fans when we walked into the gyms. We loved the outfits for this year, and we were quite in fashion as well.

One day at practice, Coach kept me on the gym floor a few minutes later than the others for a talk. I remember it well. He announced practice was over and to head to the locker room, and then he called me to wait a minute. I thought, "Oh no, I haven't had a very good day at practice, and I've disappointed him." Boy, did we hate to disappoint Coach! But instead of that kind of lecture, it was a different one. "Now, Bunny," he said, "you've got to lead the way this year. We've lost several guards to graduation, as well as Sissy from our forwards. That leaves a gap in our scoring punch, but even more so, it leaves a big gap in leadership. I'm looking to you to lead the team. The pressure will be on you this year to take up that slack in scoring. I have great confidence in you to do that. It won't be easy. Teams are out to get us every game this year, and they've seen you play for a year now. You won't have that surprise factor going for you of being a freshman. I have confidence that you can take on that leadership role, even though you're a sophomore. We've got a chance to continue to win games and championships, and you're a very important part. That's all I wanted to tell you. See you tomorrow." He gave me his trademark smile and wink, and that was the end of our talk.

Coach's words inspired me. I hadn't been thinking about filling such an important role with the Lady Vikings, but I was ready to go after it. Coach was the best at motivating players, and just those few words did it for me. I was so excited about the chance to make an impact and help the team.

A week or so before the first game on November 4th, Coach called us all into the locker room at the end of practice. Coach's meetings were always quick, terse, and to the point. He said, "Next week we start our season. Here are our goals for the year. There are three, and these are in order of importance. Number one is we want to win the State Championship. Number two is we want to win the Tri-County Invitational Tournament. Number three is we want to continue the winning streak. That's it. Think on those goals, and come prepared to play hard."

I remember thinking, "What? Our number one goal isn't to win every game and continue the winning streak?" It took a few minutes to sink in for me. The more I thought, the more I knew that Coach, of course, was right. Winning the state championship marks the ultimate success in a season, so of course it had to be our main goal. Many people would think we would spend all our time counting our winning streak games and dwelling on continuing the streak. We didn't because Coach Carter led us to work on defeating one opponent, the one we were playing at the moment. Winning every game was fun, but it was not our ultimate goal.

We were scheduled to play 12 regular season games before Christmas with eight after Christmas. In addition, we would play three games in the Tri-County Tournament if we won that championship. Our season ran from right after Halloween until right before Valentine's Day and was followed by sub-region, region, and state tournaments. Just about every Tuesday and every Friday from November until February, with the exception of a two week Christmas vacation, we had a game either in our gym or in an opponent's gym. We never had games on Saturdays during the regular season except those two weekends at the Tri-County Tournament in Manchester.

This year there were quite a few freshmen added to the roster: Edie Smith, Kathy Underwood, Carlyn Neisler, Carol Wall, Jan Hobbs, Cecilia Kendrick, and Mary Jane Robinson, and they were good players who became good friends. I'd known Carlyn since birth because we were cousins and went to church together. She was tall and thin, and Coach had her on a weight-gaining regimen. I knew Kathy Underwood from school in Reynolds, and she had talent as a guard. The others I'd not known very long, but I liked them all. Edie Smith was a standout, a member of the big Smith family that everybody knew and loved. She was smart and had a good eye for basketball strategy, and she helped Coach Carter scout one of our opponents, an important job. We rarely played a team that Coach Carter did not have some information about ahead of time, and many times he'd been to see them play himself. With our schedule of Tuesday and Friday games, and Coach's busy job as superintendent, he couldn't always see every other team play. Many times he'd send managers, statisticians, or other coaches to watch the opponents. Watching the games that closely was hard work, but Coach considered it a priority. Edie Smith says,

> "Before my ninth grade season, Coach Carter asked me to go with the scouting group to a tip-off tournament and keep some scouting charts. I had no idea why Coach thought I should go to the tournament, but naturally I went. He gave me some papers and told me he expected me to record the defenses, offenses, out-of bounds plays, and out-of bounds defenses of the teams we were watching. 'Oh, my,' I thought, 'who does he think I am?' Though I was just a thirteen year-old kid, I was determined that I would not let him down. Needless to say, I watched the game with more focus than I had ever mustered for anything in my life. I saw patterns, recognized the stimuli that created changes in offenses and defenses, and also saw individual strengths and weaknesses of players. I was writing constantly. After that time, I never looked at a basketball game in the same way."

That year, I had a very special opportunity coming up in late November, the day after Thanksgiving. During the summer I had mastered in 4-H and won a trip to the National 4-H Congress in Chicago, Illinois. This trip was a one week stay at the Conrad Hilton on the banks of Lake Michigan, traveling with the fifty or so other Georgia state winners in 4-H projects for the year. The hotel would be filled with teens from other states, and the schedule included sightseeing of the Chicago area, banquets nearly every meal, entertainment from top celebrities and companies, and fun meeting new friends from across the country. We would fly out from Atlanta on the Friday after Thanksgiving and return on the next Friday, missing an excused week of school. Of course, missing a basketball game was a worry for me. Fortunately, there was not a basketball game scheduled for the Tuesday that I'd be gone, but there was a game in Roberta the Friday that I'd fly back from Chicago. Mama discussed it with the principal and Coach Carter, saying that she and Daddy would pick me up at the airport around lunchtime, let me rest at home awhile, and get me to Roberta in plenty of time for the game that night. Of course, those plans depended on the schedules working out! Off I went on the trip of a lifetime. My first time flying (and my seat mate used the barf bag), knowing no one else on the trip that well beforehand, and visiting museums, shows, and sights around Chicago made for an interesting week. In the back of my mind was always the basketball game that Friday night, but the trip was too busy and awesome to have much time to worry. My scrapbook for that trip describes the last morning like this: "Went to bed at 3:30 am, got up at 5:30 am, left the hotel for the airport at 6:30 am, flight at 8:30 am, landed in Atlanta at 11:30 am." The travel time schedule came off without a hitch even though it was starting to snow in Chicago that morning. I was worn out, but I made it to the game in time to play, and we had an easy game against Crawford County. Many years later, I'm so thankful I took that opportunity to travel to Chicago. Though basketball was important to me, I had many other interests, and I'm grateful that I had a family and coach who encouraged me in all my endeavors.

During the early part of the 1969-70 season, our margins of victory were huge. We beat teams like Talbotton, Marion, Crawford, Yatesville, Perry, and Harris County by over 30 points. The scoring power of the Riley, Arnold, and Fuller combination was too much for opposing teams to deal with. We each could easily score 20 points a game, and it depended on who was open as to who took the shot and scored the most points. Opponents could not focus on stopping one player with a double-team or sagging defense because one of the others would take up the slack. We became great at reading the defense, and it was challenging and just plain fun. We also were good rebounders, so if a shot was missed, we'd grab it and go back up with the ball, sometimes drawing a foul. We even kidded Judy Riley that she sharpened her elbows at night in preparation for basketball the next day! She was by far our best rebounder. The three starting forwards rarely played more than two and a half to three quarters before the Rinky Dinks played the rest of that game. Rinky Dinks on the Lady Vikings got a lot of playing time, and Coach Carter never ran the score up intentionally. He'd put the Rinky Dinks in as early as the middle of the third quarter. However, we starters wanted to play, so Coach would let us play close to three quarters every game to be fair to us. It was not always easy to keep the score at a respectable margin (as we said at that time, "No brag, just fact!").

Judy Riley goes up for a basket.

I kept extensive scrapbooks during each year of my high school basketball playing days. Mama and Daddy would take me over to the Office Supply on Mulberry Street in Macon to buy one in the late summer, and I'd have the best time creating the scrapbooks as each season progressed. The Lady Vikings got a good bit of publicity because of our ongoing winning streak, so finding articles and pictures for each year's scrapbook was easy. I would, of course, have access to the Taylor County News every week, and it had many articles on all the high school activities. My parents subscribed to the Macon Telegraph, and I'd usually get the box scores and sometimes short articles from the Columbus Ledger Enquirer or the Atlanta Journal at school. I'd go to the library at school during break, get the day-old paper from the stacks, and secretly tear out the box score that our managers had called in from a pay phone. I've always wondered how I got by with tearing the day-old paper, but our librarian Mrs. Humber was a sweet lady who either didn't see it or ignored it!

After our 75th win, which was over Marion County by a huge margin, there was a blurb in the Atlanta paper that shocked me and then made me mad: "Taylor County's girls won their 75th straight last week when they whipped Marion County 68-29...Speaking of girls basketball, wouldn't it be nice if it didn't exist?!" Reading that last line hurt my heart. A huge part of my high school life would be gone if girls basketball didn't exist. I wanted to fire off a letter to the editor, but I never did. I can't say that's the only time I heard that sentiment expressed. It was a long time before Title IX put an end to such foolish statements.

Meanwhile, our coach continued to make a name for himself across the state as the press made note that the winning streak was still going strong, that Coach Carter was a master of the game, and that girls deserved a little newspaper attention. Macon Telegraph sports writer Tommy Desselle wrote a long article headlined, "Taylor County's Carter Legend in His Own Time" that describes Coach Carter's amazing record of turning out winners since the early 1960s, capturing state titles in 1966 (boys) and 1964, 68, and 69 (girls). Desselle came over to Butler to watch a practice and wrote that Coach Carter's focused practices were the key to our success. At our practice that day, Coach had the three guards working on getting the ball to the centerline against four opposing forwards. The article quotes Coach, "This drill helps our guards develop their ball handling and also makes it more difficult for them to get the ball down court." As for the forwards, the article describes how the loss of Sissy to graduation left a more balanced team with Judy Riley the top rebounder,

Fuller the best pivot player, and Arnold the best at outside shooting. Coach said, "The forwards take their keys from the guards' reactions and play accordingly. They're the best passers I've ever seen on a girls' basketball team and are extremely unselfish." Coach described the senior guards: "Denease McAbee is known as the best hustler on the team, a real fine athlete who works hard and has a burning desire to win, and Karon and Kathy Peed are top rebounders and have a sound knowledge of the game. They think well while in the game and are seldom out of position. Also, they handle the ball well. Being twins, they often confuse the opposition!" Of the juniors, Coach said Patsy Ranow was the quickest. "She has tremendous acceleration and can outrun boys the first three steps. She is also very aggressive and always wants to improve. Regina Parks is quick and strong, and does a good job rebounding." As to how the winning streak was affecting the team, senior Judy Riley said, "The winning streak puts pressure on us, but you do not have time to think about it during a game. We work real hard in practice preparing for the games ahead, but play the games one at a time." Coach Carter is quoted, "This team has the potential to be the best team I have ever coached, but they still have to prove themselves during the tournaments." Desselle ended by stating that Taylor was averaging 70 points per game this season, the most they have averaged since the streak began.

Our practices were usually quiet and serious. No one except Coach talked much, and the only other sounds were basketballs bouncing and shoes squeaking. We'd sometimes have visitors, including fans or occasionally other coaches who wanted to learn how Coach Carter ran a practice. One I remember was Coach Chuck Miller, who was a good friend of Coach Carter. He sat way up in the bleachers and took notes on a clipboard. He slipped out of the gym unobtrusively. Chuck Miller was a highly successful coach in his own right, and I imagine he picked Coach Carter's brain many times.

During the 1969-70 season, I reached that all-important sixteenth birthday, and I couldn't wait to get my driver's license. I had to pass a written test and a driving test with a state patrolman. The week the Georgia State Patrol would be in Reynolds, I spread the word to my teammates that I'd be driving to the game that night, and Daddy took me to City Hall for the exam right after school. I made a perfect score on the written test, and I confidently got in the car to drive the patrolman around the block. The whole time I was driving, I thought I was doing fine, but when we got back to City Hall, the patrolman said, "Well, you don't get your license. You never came to a complete stop at the first stop sign." I had pulled up farther than the stop sign in order to see around the parked cars at the median, and I'm sure the patrolman was right that I had never stopped completely, even though I did check that no cars were coming. I held my tears in until Daddy and I were in the car on the way home, and then I cried until we headed for the basketball game hours later. Oh, the embarrassment! I'd told everybody I'd be driving, and now I'd never get my license. I remember a long night of swollen eyes, and Coach probably wondered what in the world had happened. I was sure I'd be asked over and over whether I'd driven to the game, but the other girls heard my first reply of "No, I failed" and didn't mention it again. I was sure no one had ever failed it before. I lived through the misery and got my license the next week, with a different examiner who asked about what happened and kindly said, "That guy seems to enjoy failing young kids."

In 1970, both the boys and the girls teams were expected to make a good showing at the Tri-County Tournament in Manchester, and we did, with both teams winning the championship. All three forwards made the All-Tournament Team, and we were so proud. Buddy Dunn wrote in the Taylor County News, "The trio of forwards, Bunny Fuller, Judy Riley, and Sandra Arnold scored 201 points during the tournament. Fuller hit the nets for 100 points, Riley scored 53, and Arnold added 48. They were at their best just as they have been all year." Also, two guards, Denease and Patsy, made All-Tourney, making five for the Lady Vikings. Dunn's article quotes the Manchester Star-Mercury newspaper as questioning, "Why are schools outside the Tri-County area in the Tri-County basketball tournament?" This questioning was probably because Manchester didn't like to see their top trophies go to the same school in both boys and girls divisions! After the trophy presentation, a fan from another school came up to me and said, "You made me lose $5." He said he'd bet we'd defeat our opponent by 25 points. We beat them by 24, and I had missed a free throw in the final seconds of the game, which caused him to lose his bet! After the championship game, a reporter from the WTVM news in Columbus said he wanted to take footage of our team celebrating in the locker room. We normally didn't have any kind of locker room celebration, so we didn't know exactly what to do, but Coach Carter playfully threw a towel over Judy Riley's head. Our real celebration was driving all the way to Shoney's in Columbus for supper, a big treat. We didn't get home in time to see what the news aired, and I've always wondered if WTVM showed the footage of Judy with the towel over her head!

Illness was always a concern on a team, but, of course, Coach knew how to handle it. Coach had all of us take a flu shot at the beginning of the season, and he had the managers dole out a Vitamin C tablet each day after practice. One day during basketball season I was feeling a little under the weather. While I was in typing class, Coach Carter appeared at the door and told my teacher, "Bunny will be back in a few minutes." He told me he was taking me up to Jimmy Smith's pharmacy to see if I had a fever and if I needed any medicine. I had no idea how he knew I wasn't feeling well, but I followed him outside, hopped in his car, and off we went uptown to the drug store to see Mr. Jimmy (who was a great basketball fan). He checked my temperature, asked me a few questions, gave me some medicine, and Coach took me back to class. I was instantly well. When I got home, I asked my mother how in the world Coach Carter knew I didn't feel well that day. We finally figured out that at the teacher's lunch table, she questioned Coach Sandy Harris about the rules concerning missing a portion of the school day and still playing ball that night. Sandy passed that information to Coach Carter, and Coach made sure my illness was nipped in the bud.

As the all-important sub-region tournaments came into the near future, we started more practice of game situations. I was always amazed that other teams, at the end of close games, seemed to be running around like a bunch of chickens with their heads cut off. Had they never practiced and learned strategy for various simulated scenarios? We had well-defined plans that we'd practiced over and over. Edie Smith says of one of those situations:

> "At one point in the execution of our well-designed stall pattern, someone threw the ball away. I went and got it and brought it back to the court. Coach Carter was explaining the importance of eliminating turnovers. 'It's simple,' he snapped. 'You just cost us four points: two points that we had the chance to score, and two points that you gave them because of stupidity.' I was still holding the ball when he started guarding me. He continued to talk to us all about the importance of good decisions, quick passes, and no turnovers. He said, 'Listen, Smith, you hold it, you sit on it, you put salt and pepper on it

and eat it, but don't you ever throw that ball away.' 'Yes, Sir,' I stammered, 'Yes, Sir.' End of discussion."

Coach had a masterful way of making us learn something. At practice, he emphasized his point and we remembered it. When we got into a similar situation in a game, we were ready.

Coach's vehicle was always distinctive, and at that time his car was a bright green two-door Maverick that we could spot a mile off. Occasionally, he'd be late to practice because of his superintendent duties. We were so well-trained that we'd have already started our usual routines, the forwards shooting at the goals and the guards working on dribbling and passing drills near center court until he arrived. However, sometimes, we would relax and talk before he got there, and we'd station a look-out at the door of the gym to watch for his bright green Maverick.

One day at practice, three boys showed up. Coach announced that since our tournament opponents were going to feature faster and taller girls than we had faced all year, he had asked three of our classmates to come for some specific practice with us. He first had the boys playing against our first string guards, passing the ball quickly and setting screens for the guard out front. I think the guys were pretty amazed when they found it was a lot harder to play against those guards than they'd thought. After a while, we forwards got our turn with the guys guarding us. Playing against boys was definitely challenging, but we adjusted pretty quickly to these new opponents. Coach didn't know it then, but he picked some prestigious guys to come out and help us that day. Wayne Smith became an educator and was elected superintendent of Taylor County Schools, serving for over 20 years in that position. Chuck Byrd became a successful lawyer in the Macon area, and Ben Cheek became an OB-GYN in Columbus and has delivered many Taylor County babies.

Our region tournament was held in Thomaston that year. The semi-final game of region is the all important game that determines who continues on to the state tournament. We were playing Greenville in Thomaston, and the game was marred by poor officiating. My notes in my scrapbook say we were tied at the first quarter, ahead by 14 at the second quarter, and ahead by 19 at the third quarter before they came back and caught us in scoring. The referees called 25 fouls on us, including 19 in the final seven minutes as we lost our 19 point lead. Over the course of the game, two Lady Vikings fouled out after five fouls, and three girls, including me, had four fouls — unheard of for our team. We ended up winning 60-56, a game too close for comfort, and the closest of our season thus far. Coach Carter decided he had to take action, and early the next morning he made a call to Bill Fordham, the executive director of the Georgia High School Association in Thomaston, and asked him to attend the region finals game that night. He didn't tell him why; he just made the request. With Mr. Fordham in attendance, the officiating for the region finals was excellent, much different from the night before. We won against Pike County easily (74-59) in a fairly called game to advance on to the state tournament.

After our 90th win, Harley Bowers, the Macon Telegraph Sports Editor, produced a funny article headlined: "Norman Carter - State School Board Wasn't Impressed," describing how the State Board of Education required Coach to go back to college for a course in physical education so he could teach PE. Even though his girls teams had won four state basketball championships during his ten years in Butler and won 90 games in a row, he wasn't certified to teach a PE course, and had to take a class at Mercer University to fulfill state requirements.

Everyone who was part of the Lady Vikings team contributed to our wins, and our scorekeeper helped us get six extra points against Temple of Carroll County in the first round of the 1970 state tourney held in Fairburn. We arrived at the game and noticed that Temple had brand new, nice-looking uniforms. We hoped the new uniforms wouldn't bring them good luck. At a state tournament game, the official scorer was from a neutral place, and each team had its own scorekeepers as well. During the first quarter, our scorekeeper, Beth Jones, told Coach Carter that the numbers and players' names she received before the game didn't match for the Temple team. Coach Carter told her to tell the officials, and she did. The officials didn't want to do anything about it, so Coach Carter showed them the wrong numbers again at the half and reminded them that the rule book called for a technical for every wrong number in the scorer's official book. The officials didn't feel the mistake was Temple's fault, but then they learned that both Beth and the official scorer had gotten the numbers from the Temple scorekeeper. When we returned from the locker room after our halftime lecture, the officials called Coach Carter and the other coach to center court and conferred with them. Then Coach Carter called us into a huddle, told us what had happened, and called for senior forward Judy Riley to go with the officials and shoot the technical fouls: a free throw for each number that was incorrect in the score book. Imagine: the crowd for both sides saw our player go out to the foul line with the official, no one else on the floor. Judy shot free throw after free throw, ten total, and points were added to the scoreboard for our side. The score changed from 26-20 to 32-20. The crowd went crazy. Our fans didn't know what was going on, but they saw points being added to our score, and they liked it. The Temple fans didn't know either, but they could certainly see it wasn't to their advantage, and they didn't like it. The boos from the Temple crowd got louder and louder, and our crowd cheered just as loudly to match them. Judy ended the game with 15 points that night, and the final score was 51-38. She didn't enjoy shooting those technical fouls in front of the crowd all by herself, but her free throws helped us win the game. That event was the most unusual thing I saw during our winning streak. That game happened to be on Friday the 13th, and we were glad it turned out to be a lucky day for us!

Our loyal Taylor County fans followed us from the first game of the season to the last, and everyone's excitement bubbled over when we headed to the state tournament in Macon. Years later, Karon Peed, who was a senior in 1970, said, "I remember the caravans of cars going to the games, the shops in town closing, the signs on the windows saying 'Go Lady Vikings.' The support of the community was awesome." Coach Carter's daughter Cathy, who was 9 at the time, says she remembers the fun of traveling in motorcades to the game. "There would be lots of cars, maybe ten or twelve, all heading to the games out of town. Even though I was young, I enjoyed every minute of the games. Winning was fun!" Before the 1970 tournament, a group of fans led by Buddy Dunn and the Jaycees took out a full page in the newspaper to cheer us on. At the bottom of the page were poems and good wishes:

I've traveled many a mile
I've seen many a team;
But when it comes to Carter's Vikings
They're the best I've ever seen.

Kay and William Scott

Store hours starting Thursday
Will be most short and brief
Got to follow Carter's Vikings
Got to get a good seat.

Sonny Dunn

You've always played like champs
You've won 91 without a loss
You've proved to many a team
You truly are the boss.

Nellie and D Taunton

Listen, Norman and Lady Vikings
I know they're hard to beat
But nevertheless I confess
You'll sit'em on their conceit.

Buddy Dunn

Clothes will have to stay dirty
'Cause there's not much I can do.
The Preacher's going to Macon
And I'm going with him too.

Delle Dunn

Lady Vikings, Lady Vikings,
You are really great.
Come on loyal fans
Let's support them at state.

Cindy and Buddy Griggs
children of Clay and Adrian Griggs

To Macon with love
Good luck Lady Vikings!
Linda and Gary Windham

We believe: That Faith in the Lady Vikings will mean another State Championship for the Taylor County girls.
Taylor County Jaycees

An article came out in the Macon Telegraph about the senior guards, identical twins Kathy and Karon Peed, and the tradition by girls in the Peed family of playing basketball for Coach Carter. Coach said he considered the last name Peed as a good luck symbol because a Peed played on several of his state championship teams. The article says, "'Our sister Dondra was on the 1963 team. And our sister Janice played on the teams of 1964 and 1965,' said Kathy (or was it Karon)." Coach Carter said he could tell them apart on the court: "'Karon is two inches taller than Kathy. And if you can't see the numbers, then that's the giveaway.'" The article ends with Karon telling their plans after graduation of attending the Macon School of Nursing and the writer's imagining a patient's confusion at having two pretty and identical twin nurses. Today, Kathy and Karon credit Mrs. Jane Carter, Coach's wife, with helping them choose their career path because she took them to Macon and arranged for a tour of the nursing school. Coach Carter and Mrs. Jane's influence on his players was far-reaching.

In the 1970 State Class C Tournament held in Macon, we played Laurens County, Norman Park, and Stratford. The publicity by the Macon Telegraph had been mounting. Stratford Academy was the hometown school, and the articles and headlines were all about them. I really didn't think Stratford would make it to the finals because Cave Spring was back this year and was in Stratford's bracket, but the Macon Telegraph was already predicting a meeting between Taylor County and Stratford and was discussing an end to our winning streak when that meeting happened. Since we were in different brackets, we'd meet them in the finals if we both continued to win.

Our first game was at 2:30 in the afternoon against Laurens County, who had a senior and a sophomore who averaged in double

Bunny Fuller pivots to shoot against Stratford defender in state tournament.

figures. (Years later, that sophomore, Angie Bedingfield, was my classmate and teammate on the Lady Warriors at Middle Georgia College in Cochran.) Once again, our tenacious defense won that game for us, causing Laurens to shoot only eight of 44 from the field. Their coach said it was a cold-shooting episode, but we knew our guards had caused the problem. The Rinky Dinks saw action in the fourth quarter of this state game with the margin being 53-26 at the end.

By far the most exciting game of the 1970 state series was our game in the semi-finals versus Norman Park. Both teams had excellent coaches (Julian Grantham coached Norman Park) and were excellent fundamentally. Both teams were also undefeated for the season thus far. This Norman Park team, according to the Macon Telegraph, was "unawed by Taylor County's enviable record" of 92 straight wins and stayed right with us the entire game. After the first quarter, we were tied at nine. At the half, although Norman Park had led twice during the second quarter, the score was Taylor County 22, Norman Park 18. At the end of the third quarter, once again the score was tied at 37. Our guards were Denease McAbee, Patsy Ranow, and Kathy and Karon Peed, alternating three at a time as Coach saw fit. These girls always took great pride in their play, and their skill was evident in this game. We would not have won this one without their great defensive effort. The article by John Krueger, Assistant Sports Editor for the Macon Telegraph, quotes Coach Carter, "These referees knew the difference between a charge and a block and every call they made regarding this was correct. We were guilty of charging every time they called it on us, and so was Norman Park when they were called. Sure it was rough out there, but that's the way basketball is supposed to be played. When the girls realized that charging fouls would be called, they didn't hesitate to get in the way and stop the drive." Drawing charging fouls was a skill Coach worked on with guards extensively, using a padded mat to prevent injuries during practice, and our crew became masters at planting their feet to hold position and letting the forward run over them to get those calls. Our guards kept them from running their offense, and with flawless teamwork, we forwards were able to score when we got the ball. It was a tight contest, well-officiated, and the strategy by these two wise coaches was awesome to witness.

In the fourth quarter, Norman Park went ahead 37-39, but Judy

Riley tied the game 39-39 with a shot for us. Norman Park went ahead once again at 39-40. Judy made a free throw, and then Sandra and I each scored baskets to make it 44-40 with us in the lead. The lead continued to swap back and forth until Norman Park came back and tied the score at 49 with one minute and thirteen-seconds left on the clock. Norman Park fouled Sandra as she set up the offense, and she scored a free throw to put Taylor County back on top 50-49. That's when the play of the guards became critical. Norman Park had the ball and went into a freeze to wait for a last good shot. Their ball handlers were dribbling the ball out near the centerline. The clock was ticking down. We let them freeze the ball for about 30 seconds; then Coach Carter waved his hand from the bench, signaling the guards to get after them. I was standing on the forward's end at the center line with the best view in the house, watching the guards and watching the clock. When Coach Carter waved his hand for the guards to jump on them, Patsy Ranow scared the mess out of the girl who was dribbling. Patsy was always gritty and determined, and she sprang out at the ball handler with a quick jump. The Norman Park player was startled, and with a wild look of horror in her eyes, she committed a "walk" violation. The referee called the violation and presented the ball to the Lady Vikings, just what we wanted. Coach's strategy had worked perfectly. With twenty-five seconds left, we had the ball back and a one point lead. We froze the ball for the remaining seconds and won the game. How was the final score 52-49, a three point win instead of one point? The article in my scrapbook says that I was fouled at the buzzer and connected on two free throws with no time showing on the clock. I don't remember a thing about shooting those free throws. I'm glad I made them, but those two points were just icing on the cake. We'd already won that game, based on the strategy set forth by our amazing coach and the play of our tenacious guards, most especially Patsy Ranow.

Meanwhile, Stratford Academy's first game was with Cave Spring, our worthy opponent from the 1969 state final. We were watching because we knew how well-coached Cave Spring was, and we'd even seen reports that Cave Spring was picked to beat the Lady Vikings this year to get revenge for last year. That Stratford team pulled an upset over Cave Spring 47-42. Some said Coach Woodell of Cave Spring had sewn up his team's fate when he said earlier in the month that he didn't think Stratford Academy's defensive guards could stop his girls. The headline of the Macon Telegraph the morning after the game told the story: "I'm a Fool, Cave Spring Coach Sighs." Prior to their 5:20 tipoff with Cave Spring, he had said, "We're 20 points better than Stratford right now," and continued, "Our girls just know they'll win. Stratford's guards can't do it." By the half he was beginning to eat those words as Stratford led. After the game was over, Coach Woodell said, "I am the biggest fool in the world and you can quote me on that." In contrast, Coach Richard Reid of Stratford said he "didn't know if his guards could stand the pressure of it being so close, but they really came through out there. Did the best job they've ever done." Stratford's forwards trio, Betsy Longinotti, Anna Newton, and Jan Jones, went to work on Cave Spring and scored 18, 17, and 10 to lead Stratford past the formidable Cave Spring. The paper describes Betsy Longinotti, Stratford's senior forward who was just over five feet tall: "Little Longinotti's ball handling and free throw shooting (hitting 4-4 in the final three minutes) put the game out of reach for Cave Spring." Stratford then beat Dacula to advance to the finals.

As the Macon Telegraph had predicted, the final two teams of the state tournament of 1969-70 were Taylor County of Butler and Stratford Academy of Macon. Stratford was a premier Macon Georgia private school, and since the tournament was held at the Macon Coliseum and the Macon Telegraph was the local newspaper, they had received lots of press beforehand. Private schools were allowed to play a public school schedule, and Stratford evidently liked the competition in the public school division. The articles called Stratford the Cinderella team of the tournament since they had only been playing girls basketball for two years. I guess few private schools gave their girl athletes that opportunity at that time, and I saw an article after the season discussing how Bibb County Public Schools did not even sponsor girls basketball teams at all. Stratford had won three games in the state tournament before we met them in the finals, so they were obviously peaking at tournament time and playing well. That night, the Coliseum was filled with Stratford fans wearing yellow daffodils on their clothing. Their coach, Richard Reid, had worn one in his lapel in the other games of the tournament, and before our game the Coliseum looked like a sea of yellow with their fans following suit. A whole article in the Macon Telegraph was devoted to Stratford's superstitions. Betsy Longinotti wore three socks — two on her right foot, one on her left. The girls' order was always the same for sitting on the bench, taking layups in warmups, and eating their pregame meals. Each member of the team had started ordering the exact same foods since the state tourney began. The parents of the girls started wearing the same clothes to every game of the tournament. Those parents and fans were vocal in the early portion of the game. However, our fans came out in droves every game, so we knew we could stay right with them in the noise category and thought we could keep up in score as well.

Bunny Fuller drives against Stratford in finals of state 1970.

Stratford had never encountered a tenacious defense like our guards played, nor an offense like our Riley-Fuller-Arnold combination. From the beginning, the game was a rout. When Sandra scored to make it 8-6 with 4:25 left in the first quarter, Stratford never managed to catch us again the whole game. Our guards kept getting the ball back to us, we'd score easily, and we forwards proudly ran our forward press to perfection, which hampered the Stratford guards from getting the ball to the centerline where their forwards were waiting. As Coach had drilled into our heads, you can't score if you don't get the ball, and we three were determined to stop that ball from crossing the centerline when we could with our tenacious zone press. The article in the paper even discussed the problem Stratford had of getting the ball on the forward end. Coach said in the paper, "This was probably the best executed game during our winning streak." We had a great game and beat Stratford 68-50, an eighteen point margin for a state tournament final. Coach Carter afterwards said on the microphone as he accepted the trophy, "Stratford was the Cinderella team, but my girls were just a bunch of hard-working pumpkins who wouldn't quit."

We returned to the Alpine Lodge after the game for our post-state championship fun. Coach Carter and several others jumped in the cold pool again this year. The rest of us watched and cheered! It was another fun celebration, and we proudly carried the trophy back to Butler. We had a 94 game winning streak, and we'd grabbed the third consecutive state championship for the Lady Vikings.

A day or so later, the All-State teams were announced, and we had five chosen for this honor: forwards Judy Riley and I, and guards Denease McAbee and Kathy and Karon Peed. I was excited to be the only non-senior on the team, but disappointed Sandra was not chosen as well; she should have been. I tied with Stratford senior Betsy Longinotti as Most Valuable Forward, even though I'd scored 89 total points to her 83 and we'd beaten her team by an 18 point margin. As Coach Carter said in his acceptance of the trophy at the Coliseum, "Stratford has the second best team in the state, but I think we proved who is number one!"

In May, Coach Carter was selected Georgia High School Coach-of-the-Year. The award included all classifications in the state and was the top award in Georgia, voted on by other coaches. I just happened to see an article about it in the paper; Coach never told us of any awards he received. The article quotes Coach Carter as saying the honor was a surprise: "It is one of the very few times a girls coach has received the award."

A couple of weeks after the state tournament, a student who was working in the office came hurrying to find me. "Bunny, you have a long distance phone call in the office, and Mrs. Kennon said to hurry over and get the phone." I answered and heard a male voice saying, "Bunny, this is Coach Jack Moore of the All-American Redheads, a professional basketball team for women based out of Arkansas. We want you to come and play basketball with us." I was struck dumb for a few seconds, and then stammered, "But I've got two more years of high school." Surprised, he answered, "Oh, we thought you were a senior. In fact, we were told to recruit you by a coach in Georgia who was sure you were a senior." He went on to describe the honor of playing for his team and the adventures they had traveling from town to town, and I was pretty surprised that he talked so long because long distance telephone call charges at that time were not cheap! He said the team had so much fun traveling the country, playing basketball that they all loved, and competing against men's teams. All of them had bright red hair, and I assumed my hair color was the reason he'd asked me to join the team. (I found out later that most of the girls dyed their hair.) Playing for the All-American Redheads wasn't an option I wanted to pursue, as I had my sights on college, and I told Coach Moore that while it was flattering for him to call, I didn't think I'd ever be interested. After that call, I always enjoyed reading about the All-American Redheads, and I went to one of their games about a year later. Mama told Mr. Ed Goddard at the Goddard Grocery Store in Reynolds about my job offer, and from then on he called me the "All-American Redhead" whenever he saw me.

Off the court, times were changing. Sometime during this school year, girls were allowed to start wearing pant suits to school. Before this time, dresses or skirts were required. These dresses had gotten shorter and shorter with the styles, so I guess keeping girls from wearing short skirts was one reason for the rule change. I remember tales of one girl who, on the way to school on the school bus, basted a hem in the skirt she was wearing to make it about two inches shorter, and then on the way home, ripped that hem out. Her mother never knew she went to school all day with a very short skirt! There were rules such as the tunic of a pantsuit had to reach to the hips, but we were so glad to be released from wearing dresses every day that we all updated our wardrobes.

It was Judy Riley's senior year, so the Riley-Fuller-Arnold combination was ended. Nobody was a better team player than Judy. When Sandra and I were freshmen, she helped us learn the ropes of being a Lady Viking, and during our second year of playing together, after Sissy had graduated, we were probably the most balanced team in Georgia. Playing basketball with Judy was a lot of fun, and I knew it would be a different team the next year. We'd also lose guards Denease McAbee, and our famous twins Kathy and Karon Peed. Those player losses weighed heavily on our minds as we started thinking about the next year. There was also a big announcement that girls' basketball would change from three-on-three to rover rule. Sam Burke of the Georgia High School Association was quoted in the newspaper during the state tournament in Macon that the change was going to happen for the 1970-71 season. Sandra and I would have to learn to play defense! We were looking forward to the challenge.

We also had much more to think about as integration loomed in the future for our schools. We'd heard that good players would be coming over from R. L. McDougald, the black high school, who could help our basketball team. Meetings were starting to take place to plan for an orderly integration of the two Taylor County schools. We heard rumors that the schools might be split by sex, using the former black school for boys and the former white school for girls to make better use of the facilities such as labs and gyms at both campuses. The year ahead would be full of tremendous change, and we were all anxious about what was to come. The Board of Education and Coach Carter (as superintendent) had a big responsibility to do what was just for everyone, to meet the requirements of the law, and to make the best use of our small county's resources. As integration occurred, private academies were springing up everywhere, but the Board was hoping to keep students in the Taylor County public schools. The school system's goal was to provide a good education to all the children of Taylor County, and school officials kept that goal in the forefront through the changes that integration brought.

Of course, integration was controversial, and some community leaders, both black and white, did not like some of the changes. Coach Carter got death threats for his role as superintendent, and things got so bad that Taylor County Sheriff Charlie Wright advised Coach to send Mrs. Jane, Cathy and Trey away until the situation calmed down. The three went to Morgan, Georgia, to Mrs. Jane's parent's home while Coach stayed at the house in Butler. Nothing ever came of the threats, and Coach's family soon returned to Butler.

In preparation for integration, the federal government allocated funds for a summer educational program, and Coach signed up many of his basketball players to be aides to the teachers. Mama taught rising second graders in the summer program, working with black students for the first time, and I was her aide. I was already interested in becoming a teacher, and nobody was better able to train me than my mama. She was the best teacher ever. The children were just great, and I believe that summer helped these students and the teachers make the transition the next year. We had some interesting experiences, most involving a little boy who would decide that he'd had enough school and would run out the door heading home. Mama and I would yell for the custodian, who knew him, and he'd tackle the little guy on the way out the door or either run after him to his home, dragging him back to school. He'd cry awhile, but Mama would make class so interesting that he soon seemed to start enjoying his lessons.

During the winning streak years, we never practiced basketball during the summer. Coach felt that we needed a break, and he encouraged us to have other interests. There were a few basketball camps that teams could attend together, but Coach didn't want us to receive instruction (in his words: bad instruction) from any other coach. This approach was vastly different from today's spring and summer leagues, in which girls who sign up for basketball in high school essentially end their chances at other summer experiences. In addition to working with Mama, I attended several camps and conferences that summer. My most exciting experience was a two-week trip to Camp Miniwanca in Muskegon, Michigan, that I had won through 4-H. As the trip got closer, Mama and Daddy realized that I was the only 4-H'er from Georgia going. All on my own, I'd have to fly to Chicago's O'Hare airport, change planes for the flight to Muskegon, and catch the bus to the camp. My parents were worried such a long, complicated trip was too much for me to tackle alone. The state director of 4-H, Dr. T. L. Walton, called Mama and was quite adamant that I'd made the commitment and I needed to follow through and represent Georgia 4-H at the camp. She argued that I could not make those plane and bus changes by myself in Chicago and Muskegon, so Dr. Walton called the camp and discovered two other people going — a senior adult and a young girl who both went privately every year to Camp Miniwanca. Mama allowed me to go, and I met my traveling companions for the first time at the airport and had a great trip. The camp, on the banks of Lake Michigan, was a wonderful opportunity for this small town country girl; my two cabin mates were from Canada and Vietnam, and our days were full of hiking, swimming, camping, and learning. I returned home all by myself because my two traveling buddies ended up not coming home when I did. I was quite proud of traveling alone, and I think that experience was one of my best during high school. I've always been glad that Coach Carter encouraged us to pursue interests outside of basketball.

Before the school year began, the Macon paper published the new Georgia High School Association classifications for 1970-71. With integration, our school would grow in size, jumping from Class C to Class A. The Lady Vikings looked forward to the challenge ahead: playing against bigger schools, merging two teams together, and learning the new rules in girls basketball.

Seniors accept the state championship trophy. L to R: Kathy Peed, Judy Riley, Denease McAbee with Karon Peed behind Judy.

Winning Streak Season 4: 1970-71

As expected, the start of the 1970-71 school year brought many changes. Total integration was the law. While we'd had a few black students who chose to attend the white school before this year, we still had separate white and black schools in Taylor County. Like most of the county school districts in our area of the state, we were segregated until the federal government enforced totally integrated schools.

Looking back, I believe our basketball team was vital to the successful adjustment to integration in Taylor County schools. The basketball players and fans wanted the new situation to work because we wanted to continue to have good teams, so we made friends and made it work. I know that changing schools and becoming part of an established team was difficult for the girls from McDougald High School. Many years later in a speech at our Lady Vikings reunion, Coach Carter said:

> "In 1970-71, I saw the greatest example of profiles in courage I saw in my entire coaching career. We integrated. A lot of people didn't like it. Shirley Durham, Mary Riley, Mary Grover, and Earline Flowers had to come to us to continue their basketball careers. They didn't know what to expect, they didn't know me, they didn't know the girls on the team. They came over there, fit in, helped us to continue the streak, and I have nothing but admiration and respect. Our girls welcomed them with open arms, we came together as a team, and we continued the streak."

He then singled out the great Shirley Durham. "Shirley, I'll never forget it, honey, and I'm so proud of y'all for what you did."

After many meetings and much discussion during the previous year, the Board of Education had decided the best way to handle integration in Taylor County, at least for a few years, was to separate the schools by sex. The boys in our school system went to the former black school, and the girls went to the former white school. We didn't have enough teachers to staff the high school subject areas at two schools;

No. 55 Shirley Durham grabs a rebound from the opposing team as No. 10 Patsy Ranow backs her up.

this problem was solved by paying the high school teachers' mileage to drive the mile between schools at least once during the day, depending on their schedule. One of the most controversial decisions involved busing. This issue seems difficult to think of today, but many white parents did not want their children to ride buses with black children, particularly white girls with black boys. To avoid this problem, which would likely have caused more white flight to private schools, the Board of Education arranged for girls' buses and boys' buses. Two buses might stop at the same house if there were boys and girls in that family. For several years, busing remained a controversial issue for the schools.

While the school year started fairly peacefully for the students, it seemed the adults had lots of problems with the changes integration brought. As superintendent, Coach Carter bore the brunt of many complaints. While we didn't know at the time, we were lucky our coach didn't get shot during one particularly volatile incident. A white parent, angry that his child had a black teacher, came to the school and threatened the principal with a firearm. Somehow the principal defused the situation in the school office, but the parent left the school headed to Coach's house with his gun. The irate parent gave up when he didn't get an answer at the door, leaving our coach unharmed.

As school started, Sandra and I were watching for a girl named Shirley Durham. We'd learned she was a junior like we were, and we'd heard that she was a great ball player, that she'd spent many hours playing with the boys at the backyard basketball goals because she just didn't fit in with any girls playing. We'd lost Judy Riley from our forward trio through her graduation, and we were hoping that Shirley could fill that position and score points, get rebounds, and be a team player as well. Sandra and I had not lost a ball game in high school, and we'd played in every one of the winning streak games for two years. We wanted our winning streak to continue and knew we'd need some help to do that. When we started seeing Shirley at practice, we were convinced that she would be a great asset to the team. Shirley was an unbelievable player, a tremendous ball handler who could dribble while running at high speed, pass when it didn't seem possible, rebound by snatching the ball out of the sky, and shoot the eyes out of the goal with a natural jump shot. She was obviously a team player, too, making some unbelievable passes to me in the pivot. Adjusting to Coach Carter's method of play didn't seem to bother her a bit. She could do anything on the basketball court and had a desire to play with the Lady Vikings. We learned there were several more junior black girls hoping to join the team, namely Mary Grover, Earline Flowers, and Mary Riley, and we juniors on the team were in some classes together.

We started immediately developing friendships as we learned the new girls were as interested in us as we were in them. Like us, they were also dedicated to having a good basketball team. Our team building started the first day of practice and never seemed a problem from early on as the two teams meshed. It didn't hurt that our basketball coach was

Bunny Fuller goes up for a shot surrounded by Haralson County defenders.

also the superintendent of schools. Coach Carter was a mastermind at motivating people, and he did so with a no-nonsense approach, caring but tough. It worked with the girls basketball team and it worked with the people of Taylor County. There has never been another leader like him — before or since. The beginning of the year went smoothly, at least that I knew of, and the basketball season approached.

The rules had changed in girls basketball for this year. Instead of three-on-three, we would be playing rover rule. Simply explained, it meant that there would be four-on-four on the end with the ball, still with six people on the court for each team. Two players on each team would be designated as rovers and could cross back and forth from one end to the other. It could be the same two people or could change as the game went on. Teams didn't have to announce who the rovers were; the game just had to end up with four from each team on the end with the ball. The rule change also meant that those who'd never played offense would now shoot the ball when they were fouled, and those who'd never played defense would learn how to guard a player and play that position. While these rules sound confusing, we didn't find them difficult to follow.

We were shaping up to be a good team with plenty of substitutes at every position. Senior standouts included our wonderful guard Patsy Ranow who would fit the rover role easily, as well as Regina Parks and Dianne Kendrick who had always been designated guards. Underclassmen included Jean Jones, Kathy Underwood, Carlyn Neisler, Edie Smith, Carol Dyar, Faye Hayes, Cecilia Kendrick, and freshmen Harriet Jones and Susan Whidden.

Through all the changes we faced this year, Coach Carter's methods remained the same. He could always make each team member feel special and important. He'd watch for standouts at practice, praise anything good, and teach the skills we needed to learn. A big part of his motivation was through fear. While we loved Coach Carter, we were also just plain scared of him! Thinking back, it's hard to remember Coach Carter's actually punishing anyone, but we all wanted to avoid disappointing him. Harriet Jones wrote:

> "The power of the fear factor keeps bubbling up for me. As a freshman, I was totally intimidated by the whole team and just worked hard to keep up. The fear of having Coach Carter address me individually kept me completely motivated. Once we were

working on a drill on how to drive from the side of the foul line by stretching that first step. Patsy Ranow--a senior that year who was quick as a cat and tough as nails--was the guard that we had to drive around. The fear factor was truly working for me that day. Coach Carter said to drive around her, so I did--to the surprise of everyone, including myself. Coach Carter gave me a funny look and told me to do it again. Somehow I was successful again. He then asked me if my game uniform was so heavy that it was slowing me down in games. Of course I didn't realize the sarcasm--I just knew that I was too afraid not to do what he told me to do. You can call it fear or respect, but I know at times it allowed me to do the impossible!"

Coach Carter's Fundamentals of Basketball

As I watched Coach mold these new players into his team of veterans, I was beginning to recognize and appreciate Coach Carter's repetition of the fundamentals of basketball. I'm sure I heard him say certain phrases hundreds of times over the years I played for him.

• Shoot a jump shot. Use the backboard when you're close to the goal. That's what the painted square is for.

• When you catch the ball, jump and land on both feet. Then you can use either foot to pivot and not be called for a walk.

• When beyond the paint, always start with the ball above your head. Make a pass from there. Drive by moving the ball down the side of your body and your shoulder down, always protecting the ball from the defense. If they reach for the ball, they'll foul you.

• I can teach anybody to shoot, but it takes sense to play defense. (We forwards were always a little offended by this one!)

• Block out on defense. Block your player first by pivoting toward the goal, then look for the rebound.

• Find your spot on the free throw line at the beginning of the game, and the beginning of the half, and go back there each time you shoot. Always bounce the ball the same number of times, take a deep breath, exhale, and then shoot. Do your pre-shoot routine on every free throw you ever shoot, whether in practice or in a game.

• Cut into the pivot. Fake behind, then go in front. Fake in front, and go behind. (I loved to see Coach Carter laugh out loud at practice when I faked so well that the guard turned a circle looking for me.)

• If you miss, grab that rebound and go back up to shoot. Don't bounce the ball. Get a grip on the ball and take the defenders up with you.

• Cut into the lane for a pass. When you catch the ball in the lane, use your peripheral vision to note which side the guard is on. Pivot the other way, protecting the ball with your body, then lead with your elbow up through their arms possibly getting a foul, and make the shot.

• When under the goal, sometimes use a good fake with your head to get the guard to jump. Then as she comes down from her jump, you go up with the ball, use the backboard, and make the shot.

• Never dribble the ball when you get a rebound in the paint. Go back up with it and put it in the goal.

• The less you dribble the ball, the better off you are. Very rarely, if ever, do you bounce the ball as a pivot player.

• Use the backboard for any shot around the goal.

• I don't care if you use a steel barrette, get that hair out of your eyes.

• When guarding someone with the ball, don't look at their eyes or their head. Look at their mid section—it will tell you where they're going.

• When guarding someone without the ball, watch their eyes.

They'll telegraph when the ball is coming and you can intercept.

• You're ahead a point or two, and the other team has the ball. Play good smart defense and make them work for a good shot. Try your best not to foul.

• You're behind a point or two, and the other team is holding the ball. Make them do what they don't want to. Press the one with the ball. Close the passing lanes, and make them go toward the goal. Their coach has obviously told them to go toward the center line.

• If you have to foul one of them in order to get the ball back, know who's the worst free throw shooter on the team and try to foul her.

• Play the best, smartest, zone press when they're bringing the ball to the line. Walk through it at practice over and over until you know exactly what to do. Know your position well.

• When I'm talking to you, you look straight into my eyes. I want to know you're listening.

• Play good defense and the rest will take care of itself.

With basketball so different this year, the team needed leadership, and our seniors stepped up. Senior Dianne Kendrick was a substitute who got in games more frequently this season. She was always in the game mentally, whether on the court or the bench, and served as a great example to other players. Another senior was Regina Parks. Regina was a girl who loved hunting, unusual in those days, and I remember seeing several teachers gathered around her one day as she described the big deer she'd killed that morning. With her laid-back, friendly personality, Regina was a favorite of all of us. She usually played on the guard end of the court, sometimes roving and playing forward. Regina stood out in a quiet way.

Because of the new Taylor County busing arrangement, this year we would be traveling to away games in cars rather than on a bus, with the girls and boys teams traveling separately. Coach Carter had to arrange for cars to drive his players to the game. He usually drove the seniors in his car, and a manager would drive several players in his wife's car. A few families had station wagons with rear-facing back seats, and we loved to ride in those. Some of the usual drivers were my parents, Patsy Ranow's parents, Kathy Underwood's parents, and Jeri Harris, the cheerleader sponsor. Some parents couldn't get off work early enough to join the caravan, but somehow Coach always arranged enough cars for everyone. We'd leave from the gym and return there after the boys games.

Our first game of the year was against Marion County, and it started with a scary but inspiring incident that seemed to set the tone for our season. Pretty early in the game, Shirley Durham was injured. She made a drive to the basket and went down in the lane, grabbing her ankle in pain. Coach Carter went out immediately to check on her. He stooped down, picked Shirley up, and carried her to the bench. It was not a bad sprain, and Shirley was well enough to go back in pretty soon. When she ran back onto the court, our crowd gave her a standing ovation. It was great to see the support and care that Coach and the fans showed our new player Shirley, and it seemed to me that we all breathed a sigh of relief that we were still the Lady Vikings. I believe this incident was a turning point for Taylor County. The players, the coaches, the fans, the cheerleaders, and the managers were one cohesive unit. As senior Patsy Ranow said many years later, "The Lady Vikings had class."

No. 31 Sandra Arnold sinks a layup as No. 54 Shirley Durham watches.

The first games of the season passed quickly with easy wins.

Coach Carter never let us score over 100 points in a game during the streak, but we did score 99 against Crawford County in the second game of this 1970-71 season. With the starters only playing until half time, every girl on the team got to play. Other early wins were against Marion County, Mary Persons of Forsyth, and a region game against Pike County.

On December 8th, we were to play for our 100th victory against Manchester in Butler. The milestone game got lots of press, with articles in the Macon Telegraph and Columbus Enquirer. The Atlanta Journal sent their prep editor, Joe Litsch, who interviewed Sandra Arnold's mom as well as Coach Carter. The gym was filled to capacity with a reported 1,000 people and a couple hundred more fans around the boundaries. Barbara Arnold, who was a nurse at the local hospital in Reynolds, is quoted in the article, "This is the first year we've been fully integrated and we didn't know how it would work out, but it hasn't affected the girls at all." She said she'd heard, "Perry is really laying for us. That game is coming up in a week or so. We'll just have to wait and see." The article emphasizes Coach Carter's outstanding record, saying that since he'd started coaching girls only, he hadn't lost a game. We won game number 100 by a score of 64-33 over Manchester.

An article in the Macon Telegraph by Harley Bowers states that while we'd won our 100th game, we were still short of the state record of 118 wins by Baxley. We could reach that record during this season if we continued winning.

The 100th winning game was also covered with a short report from WMAZ Sports Anchor Bobby Pope. Having been born in Taylor County before moving with his family to Thomaston, Mr. Pope was always a fan of Taylor County. We enjoyed the publicity, but we really weren't paying any attention to records of wins or thinking ahead to reaching the streak record. As always, we were just playing games one by one and trying to win every one. We had not had a close game those first seven games of the 1970-71 season, but Perry was soon to make it exciting. We knew every team would feel like their season would be made if they could beat us, and we'd heard Perry wanted it bad.

Sandra saved our skin against the powerful Perry Panthers a couple of games later in Perry. Tommy Desselle led his article in the Macon Telegraph describing how Sandra dribbled half the length of the court for a layup that propelled the Lady Vikings to an exciting 40-38 victory in Perry. Coach Carter said, "Sandra's a great athlete and she did exactly what I told her. We got her the ball, then cleared the right side, leaving it wide open for her." Only six Lady Vikings played in the game that night; Sandra Arnold scored 12 points, I scored 20, Regina Parks scored 3, and Patsy Ranow scored 5, with Mary Grover and Earline Flowers playing guards. Shirley Durham missed the game with the flu. Coach continued, "It was one of our worst shooting nights, but Perry's defense had something to do with that. We have confidence in Bunny Fuller and kept going to her. I knew she would have to start scoring sometime." That was the thing about Coach Carter. He made me (and all his players) have confidence even when we were having a bad night. He never said, "Stop shooting for this game. You're not hitting." Instead he took me aside and said, "Keep shooting the ball. It will start going in. Don't worry about it a bit." He then gave one of his trademark smiles and winks, and I felt so much better. Coach Carter's encouragement helped me to end the game with 20 points even though I wasn't playing the best. "Defense definitely saved us against Perry," Desselle quotes Coach Carter. We had some good defenders. Mary Grover and Earline Flowers had stepped up and were getting lots of playing time while learning the flow of the game under Coach Carter. Of course, Sandra and I had to play defense when we roved. Coach alternated the rovers a lot, with the usual pairs being Sandra and me, and Shirley and Patsy. Coach Carter explained, "I don't believe the same girls can run up and down the court all night and give 100 percent the entire game. Thus, we switch according to the situation and quarter." Desselle wrote, "The Lady Vikings' confidence is perhaps personified best by senior Patsy Ranow. The petite 5-6 guard hustles every minute, comes up with more than her share of loose balls and is also a good rebounder despite her size. Miss Ranow wins the majority of her jump balls against taller opponents. She had two key rebounds and forced a pair of Perry turnovers in the hectic fourth period." The third quarter ended with the score tied at 30. Once we got ahead in the final quarter, we never trailed again. The game was tied twice, and Sandra sank two pressure packed free throws, her only free throws of the game, with one minute and eleven-seconds left, making the score 37-34. Desselle's article continues, "Fuller, who played the fourth period with four fouls, hit another big foul shot, giving her team a 38-36 edge with 27 seconds on the clock." Then Perry tied it 38 all with 20 seconds left, and next Sandra worked in for that winning layup. Our winning streak was intact, and we had a close game under our belts. The difference in the two teams goes back to our great Coach Carter working with us so much on what to do in close situations. We worked our offense without getting flustered. The article by Desselle says, "The calmer Lady Vikings prevailed."

We continued with one last game before Christmas vacation, at my favorite away gym - Manchester. I ended up with 43 points that night as those old fashioned backboards in that gym were always good to me!

Managers Joyce Kendrick and Melodie Bohler fill up gatorade bottles at the Holiday Inn.

As in years past, our managers were important to our success, and their job this year had become even bigger, with one of them often having to drive some of the team members to away games. Joyce Kendrick tells a story of an ill-advised stop at the Dairy Queen in

Manchester when she was driving some players home from the game:

"We left the gym before Coach Carter and as we passed the Dairy Queen it was like it was calling us to stop. We took a vote and decided it would be okay to get a quick snack for the trip back to Butler. We pulled in, jumped out of the car, and lined up at the window to order (this was so long ago that most fast foods were walk ups). I had my hot fudge sundae and was in the car ready to go. The others were in various stages of getting their orders, loading the car, or still in line waiting to place their order. All of a sudden, the green Ford Maverick pulls into the Dairy Queen parking lot. Coach Carter jumps out, opens the passenger side of the car, leans down and speaks these words. 'Get out, and throw those ice creams away, throw it ALL away.' Of course we followed Coach Carter's directions. I couldn't believe I had just thrown away my untouched hot fudge sundae in a trash can. He snapped to the others in line, 'Load up, and stay right behind my car, I mean right behind me, the rest of the way to Butler.' We did as instructed — those with ice cream found the trashcan to stuff their treats and those who were waiting in line left their place and jumped in the car. Off we went back to Butler staying right behind that green Ford Maverick. If it passed a car, I passed a car. The tension in our car was so thick you could cut it with a knife. We worried over what was going to happen to us and if Coach Carter would tell our parents. But most of all we were upset because we had displeased our coach. There were a lot of tears shed that night. We pulled up at the gym right behind Coach. He came over to the driver's side this time and simply said, 'What would have happened if you had a flat tire out in the middle of nowhere tonight? How would I have explained to your parents if you'd been kidnapped or worse? I had no idea where your carload was, whether it was ahead or behind me, or that you had stopped. I hope you've learned a lesson.'"

That was just one of many lessons we learned from Coach Carter.

During our two week holiday break, we had a couple of practices during the week after Christmas. For my upcoming January 1st birthday, Daddy and Mama took me and two close friends to see the All-American Redheads play in Warner Robins. One of the referees recognized me and brought three players over to meet me during half-time. These ladies were a good team of ball players who loved basketball and had smiles on their faces the whole game. Based out of Arkansas, their team traveled around in a long, flashy limousinc. They played men's teams in local communities, usually as a fundraiser for a community organization. They were dressed in red, white, and blue stripes, knee pads, horizontally striped socks, and high top Converse All-Stars, and their hair seemed all colored out of the same bottle of bright red hair dye. My friends laughed and said my naturally red hair looked washed-out next to the team members' hair. Although I never had interest in playing for the All-American Redheads, it was great fun to watch a professional women's team.

As basketball started again after the break, I just could not get back in the groove in the early games of the new year. In my scrapbook, I wrote about our first game against Marion County, "I played a sorry game. Got yelled at, too." While Coach Carter would never get in players' faces and humiliate us during a game, as I've seen some coaches do, he would not let us get by with poor playing, and I faced some tough practices after the Marion County game. My slump continued over the next games. Against Villa Rica I only scored 12 points with Sandra and Patsy taking up the slack, scoring 17 and 16 respectively. I finally started playing better at my favorite gym in Manchester as we began the Tri-County Tournament with a win.

The challenges of integration were brought home to me in an incident after our first game in the tournament. While we waited for the Taylor County boys game, some of us went to a restaurant across the street for a burger. As we started to walk in the restaurant, I felt someone grab my arm hard and tug me back. It was Mary Riley. "Bunny," she said, "you reckon they let blacks in this restaurant?" I looked into her anxious eyes and felt a chill as I thought how awful it was for Mary to have this worry, something I'd never even considered. I said, "I don't know, Mary, but if they don't you and I will walk back over to the gym. Let's go see." We headed for the door then, and the waitresses let us in with no comment. The crisis was over, but it gave me a feeling I'll never forget and brings tears to my eyes even today.

As we'd gotten to know each other over the course of the year in the classroom and on the basketball court, friendships developed between the white and black players, particularly among my junior classmates. Of course, Sandra Arnold, Jean Jones, and I had been friends, classmates, and teammates for years, and Shirley Durham stood out to me because, as forwards, we practiced together every day. Shirley's laugh was infectious, and she and Jean had nicknames for each other: Shirley was "Turtle" and Jean was "Tippy Toes." Earline Flowers and Mary Grover were two guards who were as dependable as the day is long. Mary Riley had a fiery temper, but she was fun to watch play the game and was getting better with every game. Coach was trying to develop her defensive skills so she could help us with some of the taller teams we'd be playing. Both in

Patsy Ranow, Mary Grover, and Dianne Kendrick rebound.

games and in the classroom, we were learning more about each other.

Little did we know that the most exciting game of the entire streak was to come on Tuesday, January 19th, in Warner Robins. Coach scheduled our Class A team against the Class AAA Demonettes to give us a challenging opponent in preparation for the upcoming tournaments. With our 108 game winning streak riding on the results, the game went into two overtimes, the only overtimes during the entire streak. Tommy Desselle wrote in the Macon Telegraph, "Taylor's Norman Carter and Robins' Sid White, two of the best basketball minds in the state, matched skills... [The] taller Demonettes were superbly prepared for an upset and might have pulled it off against a sextet with less pride and spirit. However, the Taylor County Lady Vikings have not won that streak of games by giving up the towel when behind."

We were behind 32-23 with five minutes and 42-seconds left in the fourth quarter of the game. Coach Carter told me many years later, "I looked at the scoreboard and wondered, if we'd only scored 23 points in the whole game so far, how could we catch up in the few minutes remaining?" Miraculously, our defensive press, quick layups, jumpers, and foul shots enabled us to catch them at 34-all. Both teams had chances to win in regulation play. We had the opportunity for one last shot with the game tied, but we lost the ball with 12 seconds on the clock and that gave the Demonettes a last shot. I remember watching the ball roll around the goal and fall off the side at the buzzer to leave us tied 34-34 at the end of regulation. In the first overtime, the lead passed back and forth, and we led 42-40 with five-seconds left when Robins forward Janice Murphy scored on a rebound to tie it up as the buzzer sounded. We began the second overtime, and Desselle wrote, "Both teams led by a point before Fuller's layup made it 46-45 with 44 seconds left. Guard Patsy Ranow stole the ball with 34 seconds remaining and Sandra Arnold sank one of two free tosses at the nine-second mark, ensuring the win." We'd made it through our only overtimes in 108 games, facing not one but two overtimes. It had been a harrowing night in Warner Robins for us, but game number 109 was in the books! We were a little numb for a while, and then we looked back with amazement that we'd won. I wrote in my scrapbook, "It sure was a close call — almost too close!"

We continued to the Tri-County Tournament semis and finals after that harrowing game with Warner Robins. We won the tourney easily, and Sandra, Patsy, Shirley, and I were selected as part of the All-Tourney team.

The Houston County teams of Warner Robins and Perry both came to Butler for our second games against them, and we beat both. These were hard fought games, but nothing like the two pointer and the double overtime we'd had with each earlier in the season. We were glad to get those games under our belt right before tournament time. Coach Carter said in an article before the game, "I'm picking Warner Robins to win the State AAA championship this year. Perry should also be a contender in AA." In the Houston County newspaper, Coach Bob Morrow thanked his fans for following the Perry teams the 40 miles or so to Butler. He said about 400 were in attendance, making a capacity crowd in our 1000 seat gym, and that the Perry fans gave the girls a standing ovation after it was over. I think the ovation was because of an unusual shot at the end of the game. A Perry player hit a long shot from right past the center line as the buzzer went off; the shot was spectacular, but we still won by ten points. I got a good laugh out of Coach's quote in the paper, "When you are guarding Bunny Fuller, she's like trying to grab hold of a greased eel."

Atlanta Journal Staff Writer Ron Hudspeth traveled to Butler and wrote an article about the winning streak titled, "It's 'Basketball Tonight' With a Female Touch." The article describes our small county's sleepy, rural atmosphere, including barns emblazoned with "See Rock City," rusty Royal Crown Cola signs, and the Trailways Bus Station in the center of town. Once he settled in to watch the game, I think he was a little in awe. One paragraph reads, "The Taylor County girls are not ordinary young ladies when it comes to basketball. They play the game with a vengeance that would make the Milwaukee Bucks sit up and take notice." He was also amazed by our support in the full gym, noting the signs around the gym saying, "Rebound Regina," "Sink it Shirley," and "Blast 'em Bunny." The article quotes Coach Carter, "It's a pretty complicated thing to explain how you put a winning tradition together. But, mainly, we don't miss any of the good athletes. It's a big honor to play and make the team here." Coach admitted that the stress created by the streak was "getting pretty rugged. The pressure is beginning to tell a little bit." I read Hudspeth's description of me over and over: "Bunny Fuller, a 5-10 redhead with an amazing touch in the pivot, scores 30 points." A picture of the team huddled around Coach Carter is captioned, "Losing is an unknown quantity to Taylor County."

United Press International picked up the story of the Lady Vikings' winning streak and interviewed Coach Carter, Patsy, and me. We were used to our own local paper, local papers of the teams we played, and maybe Columbus or Macon, sometimes Atlanta, writing about us, but it was a big deal when UPI called us! "We haven't lost a game since March 1967," Coach Carter told them. "Some people talk about girls being hard to handle but I don't believe it. Most of them are afraid of me. . . I don't tolerate a lackadaisical attitude." I said, "Coach Carter is the best coach in the state and that's why we win," and Patsy echoed that sentiment. This UPI article was in newspapers all over the country; we even heard from a former resident of Taylor County that she saw it in her Pennsylvania paper.

The sub-region and region tournaments this year were unusual in that sub-region games were back to back from Monday until Thursday with region Friday and Saturday, and the games were a long way off in the Northeast part of the state. Sub-region was in Fayetteville and region in Rockmart. Because we ranked first in the sub-region, the Lady Vikings did not play until Thursday's finals. Coach got permission from Fayette County High for us to practice in their gym on Monday since we'd never played there. We were to leave during school and practice an hour or so, then return home. As we were arranging rides for everyone to Fayetteville, Coach said, "Bunny, you drive the Galaxy." I was surprised, and got up my nerve to say, "Coach, I'd rather not drive." He paused in what he was doing and asked, "Why?" "Because I'm afraid I'd have a wreck or something," I answered. He looked me right in the eye and said, "You'll drive." So we started up the curvy, hilly two-lane road to Thomaston on the way to Fayetteville. I was last in the line of cars, and as luck would have it, I got behind a log truck that could hardly pull the hills. I was scared to pass the truck at the few chances I had, and I fell behind the group. When my car finally got to Thomaston, the other cars were pulled over waiting. A girl ran back and said, "Bunny, Coach Carter said to keep up." After that warning, I just put the pedal to the metal and followed right on the tail of the car in front of me. I decided

I'd rather have a wreck than make Coach Carter mad! We practiced in the Fayetteville gym, and when we went home, Coach Carter replaced me with another driver.

In addition to our trip to practice in Fayetteville, we also made a scouting trip to watch Haralson County, so we were busy even though we didn't play until Thursday. We played a very good Haralson County team in the finals of sub-region. I wrote in my scrapbook that early in the game, Patsy Ranow and I got confused about the score, thinking we were ahead when we were really trailing. We thought we were listed as Home on the scoreboard, but we were listed as Visitors. We didn't realize we were behind until the score was 9-18. The Taylor County News says, "Haralson County of Buchanan jumped out to a quick lead and went out at half-time with a five point lead. But the Lady Vikings, champs as they are, gained the lead in the fourth quarter and turned back the determined Rebels - winning by a score of 55-53." With this 118th win, we tied the state record for consecutive wins set by Baxley in the 1940s.

The region tournament was in Rockmart (132 miles from Butler) the next night, so after our sub-region championship, we headed for the Holiday Inn in Rome. As we drove that night, our caravan of cars had a disaster when a chain reaction wreck occurred. No one was hurt and the cars were barely damaged, but it did cause a delay, and we arrived at the Holiday Inn very late. Coach had asked to get in the Rockmart gym on Friday to practice, but it was in use, so we set up our own outside gym. The managers taped off a section of the parking lot at the motel, and we ran through our offense and defense right there. Despite our car wreck, late night, and makeshift practice, we played well that night and set the state record at 119 consecutive wins with our win over Model 53-29. We were proud, but we didn't have time for celebration or fanfare. We had a region tournament to win.

The region championship game was against Cartersville, a tall team with two six footers. I remember this game from a personal level because it was the first time I'd ever led a fast break. I grabbed the ball on their end with a rebound and started dribbling. Some nights I could dribble and some nights I couldn't. I had not tried to dribble that often because it was a cardinal rule of Coach's not to bounce the ball if you didn't have to. This was a night when I could handle the ball unusually well, and I went right past everybody from one end of the court to the other and then stopped for a short jumper. I sneaked a look at Coach, and he was dumbfounded! I also remember that Coach complimented me on a maneuver at the end of the game when we had forged ahead and I kept pressure on their team bringing the ball up the court. He said, "I didn't tell you to do that, but that was exactly what you needed to do." Boy, we lived for a compliment from Coach! Cartersville had a good team, but we pulled it out 57-54. That Cartersville game was one of the top three games this year so far, the others being the Perry game by two points and Warner Robins with double overtimes. State was ahead in Macon.

Our first game at the Coliseum this year was against Vidalia, and it was a tough one. Our zone press, usually a great strength for us, just did not work this night, and Vidalia stayed right with us in score. One of the main reasons we had trouble was that Patsy Ranow had to miss the game with the flu. We missed her so much this night, but we managed to come out on top. Regina Parks roved with Shirley, and Dianne Kendrick did a capable job of supplying guard power with Earline Flowers and Mary Grover alternating. The margin of 57-40 doesn't look close, but for 22 minutes Vidalia gave us a good run, leading at the end of the first quarter and the third quarter. We caught up at 31 all in the fourth, and then the paper says "Taylor County romped for the final six minutes." Coach Carter told us he blamed our poor play on himself and said that we were going to the gym when we got home to correct what went wrong. There was not a single question from parents about why he was taking us to the gym at 9:30 that night after the game. We all knew we wanted the next game, and we had to be prepared to do better. Every game at State is a championship in its own right because if you lose your season is over. I remember hitting the bed about 11 that night, tired but feeling better about the next game.

Even though we won the next day against Putnam County 44-22, Coach Carter was not pleased with our play. To most the game looked like an easy win, but when Coach felt like we weren't playing well, the score didn't matter. He said our defense was better but we were still not playing as we should on offense. Sandra had jammed her thumb early in the game, and it always made me anxious when the Fuller-Arnold combination wasn't up to par. We had several crucial turnovers on the offensive end of the court, and Coach did not like turnovers. Despite the turnovers, we got way ahead and the

Rinky Dinks got in this game near the end. The sweetest story came out of the game for freshman substitute Susan Whidden: "My future husband says he fell in love with me while I was shooting a free throw during the state play-offs at the Macon Coliseum!"

We headed into the semi-final game against a great Miller County team with some doubts, but with Patsy Ranow back up to full speed. Her assignment: keep their great pivot player from scoring. Coach said their pivot forward was at least as tall and strong as he was, while Patsy was only about 89 pounds soaking wet, but Coach had a strategy. He told Patsy he'd watched the Miller County girl play, and every time she cut into the lane to get a pass, it was always in front of her guard. She never went behind the guard. He told Patsy, "Every time she tries to cut in front into the lane, you jump in front of her, let her run into you, and hit the floor to get a charging foul." The guards had worked on drawing charging fouls so many times at practice over the years that we knew Patsy could do it. Miller County came out roaring in the first quarter. Their confidence didn't last long as Patsy did her assignment perfectly, frustrating the pivot forward when she couldn't cut into the lane without a charging foul. The pivot player soon had three fouls on her and had to sit out a while before half time. Patsy told us later that, because she was so small, her mother had to take up her uniform and left the extra material in the back. That night, with all her falls on charging fouls, she was grateful for the extra padding on her behind! We silenced Miller's explosive play and swept past the semi-final round of State 53-37. Our zone press was working better this game, causing Atlanta Constitution columnist Tom Dial to write, "Don't expect to see a spectacular show from Taylor County unless you like spectacular defense, for that is Taylor's 'thing' — defense. It is, more often than not, a moral victory for the opposition to merely get the ball across the centerline. Taylor is that tenacious." However, we knew we'd have a tough opponent in our final game. Dial wrote, "Berkmar, which has matched Taylor's 28-0 record for this season, will not be a pushover."

The headline in the Macon Telegraph says, "Taylor Girls Want No. 4" and I wrote beside the clipping in my scrapbook, "Sure do!" We played our best game of the state tournament against Berkmar High School from Gwinnett County. I remember that game as one in which everything worked. We started off by posting 12 points

Players and cheerleaders lead the crowd in chanting, "Four in a row!" L to R: Regina Parks, Shirley Durham, Susan Whidden, Carlyn Neisler, Bunny Fuller, Edie Smith, Sherry Parks, Carol Dyar, Dawn Pennington, Melodie Bohler.

before Berkmar even scored. An article in the Telegraph after the game reads, "Fuller hit a brilliant 10 of 11 field goal attempts." I didn't realize during the game I was shooting that well. I ended with 22 points. Shirley Durham added 10, most on shots from between 20 and 25 feet out, and I remember many excellent passes to me in the pivot from both Shirley and Sandra Arnold. Sandra was right behind Shirley with 9 points scored. Patsy Ranow and Regina Parks spearheaded our man-to-man defense, making numerous steals and rebounds. The Berkmar coach is quoted in the paper, "We got off to a slow start but we couldn't have played any better basketball than we did in the second half. But even that wasn't enough the way Taylor was hitting from the field." We Lady Vikings just had an all-around great game, and it was the best time to have it. The game ended with Shirley and Sandra putting on a ball handling exhibition to freeze the ball. We were ahead by six, and Coach said the two of them had Berkmar's girls "running in circles." The clock ticked down, and we won the State Championship of 1971 by a score of 49-43.

We had five girls on the All-State team. Seniors Patsy Ranow and Regina Parks were selected as guards, and juniors Sandra Arnold, Shirley Durham, and I were selected as forwards. Patsy was chosen Most Valuable Guard in the state, and I was selected Most Valuable Forward for the second straight year. Of major note was that the seniors this year - Patsy, Regina, and Diane - had not lost a single game during their entire four years of varsity basketball. The Macon Telegraph said, "These Taylor County senior girls hold a distinction that few players in the nation — prep, college or pro — can match."

We had won state in three classifications now, one in B in 1968, two in C in 1969 and 1970 and now one in A in 1971. Our fans all raised their hands with the thumb held in to show four fingers and chanted "Four in a row" as Coach accepted the State Championship trophy. He asked the crowd if they'd like to see 200 wins in a row, and cheers went up. We ended the year with a 30-0 season and a 124-0 winning streak.

Coach Norman Carter accepts the State Championship trophy as Patsy Ranow and Carol Dyar hold it aloft. L to R: Harriet Jones, Sandra Arnold, Edie Smith, Carol Dyar, Patsy Ranow, Debbie Johnson, and Coach Carter.

That summer, Coach Carter started his own basketball camp, Norman Carter Basketball School for Girls, on the campus of Tift College in Forsyth. With the success Coach Carter had with girls basketball, starting a basketball camp was a natural step for him. Unlike most basketball camps at that time, Coach Carter's camp was not for teams, but for individual players. He offered two one-week sessions, and both were full. The campus at Tift College had dormitories, a cafeteria, a swimming pool, and a big gym. Coach invited Sandra and me to each attend one of the two sessions offered, so she went the first week and I went the second. Sissy and Judy Riley were counselors at the camp. The week I went, several of the Perry girls were there, including Luann Thompson, Debbie Murphy, and Lynn Lawson. These great players were friendly but competitive. Perry had been one of our fiercest opponents this past season, and I knew they were on our schedule for my senior year.

The first few days at camp were rough because the weather was so hot, and after practicing all day, going up and down the stairs to our second-floor rooms was miserable. We learned that jumping up and down the stairs was easier on our tired, sore muscles. After a few days, we adjusted and felt better. I particularly remember the scrimmage game we had the last night of camp, with the three Perry girls on one team and me on the other. Even though it was just a scrimmage, I couldn't help being competitive, and if there was a clock and a score kept, then it was a game I wanted to win! We were close, with the lead changing back and forth throughout the game. In the closing seconds, my team was behind by two. We had no coach for these scrimmages, so I just took on the coaching job and called time-out to tell my teammates what to do: steal the ball or foul so we'd get the ball back for a chance at tying the game. The coaches refereeing looked at Coach Carter to see if he wanted to let us have a time-out since this wasn't a real game. He smiled and signaled to go ahead; I guess he wanted to see what I'd do! We got the ball back on a turnover by the opponents, and I called time-out again to set up a final play. I heard one of the coaches working the camp remark, "Bunny knows what to do in a close game situation better than I do!" I'd learned from the best. We'd spent many minutes of practice working on the last few minutes of close games.

As always during summer, I pursued other interests besides basketball. That summer, I went to Miami with our school's state winning parliamentary procedure team for the national competition at the FBLA Convention. The parliamentary procedure team was probably the second-best known team from Taylor County (after the basketball teams, of course), having won state and national many years during Mrs. Edyth Guy's long business-teaching career. Parliamentary procedure refers to the correct way to run a business meeting, and we studied Robert's Rules of Order and held practice meetings once a week for most of the school year. We won first place at that national competition and capped it off with a cruise to the Bahamas.

I know I was pretty lucky to get to take lessons, go to camps, and travel so much. I once asked my mother how she and Daddy came up with the money for me to participate in all that I did, and she responded, "Somehow, it just always appeared!" I still don't know how they did it, but I'm grateful.

No. 32 Dianne Kendrick, with No. 55 Shirley Durham and Mary Grover, battles for rebound against Berkmar in state finals of 1971.

No. 55 Shirley Durham drives for a basket.

Winning Streak Season Five: 1971-72

As the 1971-72 school year began, some integration issues were causing tension. The year began with a school boycott by some of the black students in protest of the way the buses were segregated by sex, with only white drivers for the girls' buses and black drivers for the boys' buses. Led by members of the community, this boycott continued for days, and I was getting worried because Shirley Durham had not attended school. I knew there had to be some kind of limit on the days she could miss and still be allowed to play on the basketball team. One day I saw Coach Carter in the hall and got up my courage to ask him. He replied that after a few more absences, the boycotting students would be ineligible to participate in extracurricular activities or graduate. The situation was volatile, and I know it was difficult for Shirley to be in the middle of it. Fortunately, she and others returned to school before the attendance policy kept her off the team.

Another controversial issue occurred early that school year when my class met to discuss plans for the graduation ceremony. We had an argument over what color gowns we would wear, with the black students wanting dark blue gowns while the white students wanted white gowns. To try to settle the issue, our faculty sponsor took a vote. It was an exact tie down racial lines, and we had a heated argument. The teacher didn't know what to do, so she left the gown color undecided. Immediately after the meeting, we went to basketball practice with the black and white seniors not speaking to each other. Coach, with no idea of the argument, set us to work on our offense; Shirley and Sandra were to work the ball into the pivot to me. Shirley grabbed the ball above her head, I cut into the lane, and she threw it so hard the six or so feet to me that I just jumped out of the way rather than get hit by that blazing hard ball. The ball hit the brick wall behind the court with a resounding whap. We stared at each other without a word, and Coach recognized that something was up. He called practice off soon after, and apparently investigated the problem immediately. Always a mastermind at defusing a situation with a quick decision, Coach had our faculty sponsor announce during homeroom the next day that seniors could choose to wear either white or blue gowns for graduation.

While Coach's compromise kept the gown issue from growing out of control, school was never quite the same for my class afterwards. After the argument over graduation gowns, coming on the heels of the boycott, I guess many faculty members were afraid of controversy and didn't volunteer to lead clubs and activities. Bad situations couldn't happen if no activities were allowed. My senior class missed out on many traditional rites of passage. We had no high school annual, no homecoming festivities, and no school-sponsored prom. I discovered years later that our class roster was not even listed in the Taylor County history book, *Taylor County Turns Back the Clock,* published by the *Taylor County News* in 1976. The book lists graduates for each year of Taylor County High School from 1966-70. Then it states: "After the change to Girls and Boys Schools, no lists were available for three years." After being segregated for so many years, integration came with challenges, and it was not successful overnight. Basketball helped ease the strain by giving us a common focus.

Every student participating in basketball had to have a physical, and Coach made arrangements for all of us to get one in Reynolds from Dr. Whatley. The six seniors, Sandra Arnold, Shirley Durham, Earline Flowers, Mary Grover, Mary Riley, and I, went in Mrs. Jane's navy blue Galaxy. As we traveled, we listened to the radio and talked about school. Then someone asked, "Do y'all ever wonder what it will be like if we lose a game?" I couldn't believe that thought had been spoken aloud. I always knew if doubt ever entered our minds, we could very possibly lose a game. For four years now, including the three years that I'd played on the team, we never had lost. All those regular season games and tournaments, at least 30 games a year, had been in the win column. During the previous season, we had passed both the 100 straight mark and the former state record of 118 wins. We would start the season this year with the streak at 125. I was a senior this year, and I didn't want to lose a game. I wanted to win for my team and my coach. I wanted to end the season with a perfect record, just like the four years before this one.

There were more seniors on the 1971-72 Lady Vikings than there had been any other season during the streak. As always happens during any student's graduation year, the group started thinking of the "lasts" that were occurring during basketball season, including our last first home game, our last Tri-county Tournament, and our last regular season game. Schedule cards, sponsored by Walker's Grocery and Smith's Pharmacy, came out in early fall. Games started November 12th and would be played every Tuesday and Friday until around Valentine's Day. There were familiar teams on the schedule: our adjacent counties like Marion County, Crawford County, and Talbot County, as well as the big competitive schools from Houston County, namely Perry and Warner Robins. We were in the same region as last year, with teams from far away like Haralson County, Fayette County, Villa Rica and Carrollton. We had an occasional Saturday night game this year because of our region teams being so far from Butler.

No. 35 Bunny Fuller and No. 31 Sandra Arnold never lost a game in the Taylor County gym and played in every game from their ninth grade year through their senior year.

Marion County was traveling to Ellaville to play a game before we started our season, so Coach gathered several of us to go to the game. He sent us up to the bleachers with clipboards and charts, and we studied their offense and defense. We were watching for whether the team played man-to-man defense or zone and how they handled screens. We noted any unusual out-of-bounds plays or zone presses. Coach Carter had us keep shot charts on the players we'd be guarding, watching whether they always drove to their right or left, or whether they cut in front or behind the guard in the pivot. They had several good players, including a six-footer that I would be guarding when I roved. It was always interesting to watch a game with Coach and then hear what he said about the team in practice. He used what he learned about their players and their offensive and defensive tendencies to prepare us for the game. We beat Marion 65-43. Our next game was at Crawford County, and Perry was scouting us. Because the scouts were there, Coach pulled an interesting stunt by changing our offense and only having the first string play the first half of the game. The Rinky Dinks played the entire second half. We won by 28 points over Crawford County that year, and Perry's scouting this particular game probably didn't help them too much.

During Thanksgiving holidays, we practiced on Saturday and Sunday because Warner Robins was coming to Butler on the Tuesday after the holidays. It would be their first game of this season. Warner Robins was the team that we'd played two overtimes against the year before, and they were runners-up for the State AAA title. Everyone expected the game to be close, and it was. A huge crowd was there in Butler, packed into the bleachers with standing room only. I roved the entire game without a break, a first for me, because we needed my height for rebounds and defense against those tall girls. My defense was nothing to brag about as I guarded Jeannie Mobley, who got 22 points. She was joined by her teammate Janice Murphy (who would become my teammate a year later at Middle Georgia College) with the same amount of points. As for our offense, the Macon Telegraph article the next day said the Demonettes "shackled Sandra Arnold" who got only three points, much lower than her usual. I scored 38 points, and Shirley Durham added 21 to take up the slack. We won by four in a pretty high scoring game, 67-63, making the streak 127 games in a row. The Daily Sun, the newspaper out of Warner Robins, referred to our gym as "Heart Attack Alley" and said the game matched two of the state's top girls' coaches in Sid White, the veteran coach from Warner Robins, and our Coach Norman Carter.

Meanwhile, I saw in the papers that the other great Houston County team, Perry, was winning its first two games by huge margins, 88-52 and 94-29. I'd had the opportunity to meet Luann Thompson, Debbie Murphy, and Lynn Lawson at basketball camp the summer before, so I kept up with them as the season progressed. We also scouted Perry when they played Northside of Warner Robins in early December. I had the assignment of watching Luann Thompson, who I would be guarding in the upcoming game with Perry in Butler on December 10th.

I was thankful someone else got to guard their aces, Debbie Murphy, who scored 36 the night we were watching, and Vivian Brown, their ball handler and passer.

Perry had a different philosophy from ours about embarrassing an opponent. They beat Mary Persons the next game of their season 106-11, and I felt they ran up the score. The game was on the Tuesday night before we played them in Butler on Friday. The box score in the Macon paper listed only nine players from Perry as getting in the game. Our coach would never allow us to run up the score against an opponent. We starters rarely got to play an entire game. The fourth quarter usually belonged to the Rinky Dinks.

With the issue of the graduation gowns resolved, relations among the seniors were better, and Shirley Durham and I continued our friendship. She'd occasionally call me on the phone to talk about the next game, and once she told me that she'd probably be late because she didn't have a ride. I wondered if she was testing me to see if I'd really stop by for her and let her ride with me to the gym. Of course I did. We both had typing classes, and I sat in the seat where she sat the period before. She'd often leave me a note about the next ballgame, and I saved the one from December 8th, 1971 in my scrapbook. It was a piece of typing paper cut in four pieces and taped together. The front said "The Durham Telegraph, issue 2." The headline on the next page was "How to Win Over PERRY." The article said, "These are the things the Vikings have to do to win over Perry: 1. Tie No. 12 to a tree. 2. Cut Brown's legs off. 3. Chock no. 20's eyes out. 4. Cut no.10's arms off, and 5. Burn Murphy's toes off OR 6. Just go and get them as our coach is always telling us, and I quote: 'Play good defense and the other will take care of itself.' See you tonight! Good Luck! I always enjoyed looking for an issue of The Durham Telegraph. Shirley and I had a lot of fun.

Perry came to Butler on December 10th without having lost a game yet this season, and their defense was awesome that night. I wrote in my scrapbook, "Worst game I've ever played. Lousy defense, lousy zone press, and especially lousy offense." I only scored 10 points, and I put in parentheses that I'd played better against Perry in 9th grade when I'd scored 11 and 13 points. Fortunately, Sandra played an excellent game and scored 26 points, with Shirley scoring 14 points. Kathy Underwood was getting the starting position a lot this year, and she played some great defense, along with seniors Mary Grover and Earline Flowers. Another junior, Edie Smith, saw action at the forward substitute position and fit right in. The picture in the Perry newspaper shows a huge amount of people in the stands, from babies to senior citizens. Perry's Coach Bob Morrow is quoted, "I am still not convinced Taylor County has a better team than we do." I was glad to hear the final buzzer on this game, with us ahead 56-51.

After this Perry game, our 130th consecutive victory, a news

Bunny Fuller takes a jump shot vs. Perry in the Taylor County gym.

article came out describing Coach Carter as young, handsome, and fashionable: "For the game with Perry, he was resplendent in maroon bell bottoms, a colorful shirt, and the appropriate tie. From a distance, Carter looks much like a high school senior whose classmates voted him their 'best dressed' award." We were proud to have such a young, good-looking coach, and it's amazing to think that Coach Carter was not even 40 during our winning streak. The article also describes Coach Carter's actions during the game, from smiling when one of us made a good shot, to staring at the floor when an opponent stole the ball, to nervously playing with a towel during anxious moments. Since we players never watched Coach Carter during a game, the article's description was interesting. The article concludes by questioning how long the winning streak would continue: "Hometown fans say forever. They say if the Butler girls can't outplay another team they will simply outclass them. Perhaps they are right, but some followers of girls basketball say the end is in sight. They say it will come on the oak boards of Perry or Warner Robins, and maybe at both places."

Over Christmas vacation, with our winning streak at 132-0, the Columbus Ledger Enquirer published an article with a great picture of Sandra walking away from the camera holding a stack of school books under one arm and a basketball and her John Romaine pocketbook under the other. The four column article starts off by asking, "Would you believe a 132-game winning streak? Such skeins are unheard of in sports or any other form of competition, whether it be basketball, football, marbles, badminton, or arguments with your kid brother." One thought from Coach caught my eye. He said that he believed the winning streak gave us a psychological advantage over other teams, and that a team would probably have to be 20 points better to beat us. The article goes on to describe the Fuller-Arnold combo: "Leading Carter's Vikings are two girls who have started every game since they were freshmen in 1968-69. Since they weren't old enough to play for the 1967-68 state championship outfit, they have performed in 'only' an even 100 of the 132 consecutive victories. However, their personal winning streak is 114 since they won 14 straight games playing together on the Reynolds Junior High girls' team as 8th graders." The article praises the entire team, and ends with a quote from Coach: "They're an exceptional group of kids."

We had four practices during the second week of Christmas vacation and headed back to school on Monday, January 3rd, with the first game of 1972, a Tuesday night game in Perry, looming in our minds. Perry was a good team, and we knew their number one goal was to beat us.

That fateful game started smoothly, with us having a 12 point lead at the end of the first quarter, 17-5. By halftime, we were ahead fourteen points, 29-15. Fourteen points ahead! However, the third quarter saw a turnaround, with Perry scoring quickly and narrowing our lead to six points by the quarter's end. We lost our momentum during that third quarter, mainly due to foul trouble. Shirley Durham fouled out, and I got three fouls, with only two left before I would foul out. It wasn't until the fourth quarter that Perry went ahead for the first time in the game at 39-40 with six minutes to go. The lead went back and forth in the final minutes: we tied the score at 42, Perry went ahead, and we tied it again at 46. But then Perry took the lead again, and we couldn't get it back. I fouled out with fourteen-seconds left. I remember sitting on the bench and watching the clock tick down. At that point, I knew we couldn't catch them, and I just wanted the nightmare to end. It did. The buzzer sounded and our streak was over, with Perry beating us 48-53.

We went straight to the locker room. According to the Houston County newspaper, "The boys game had to be delayed 30 minutes as near pandemonium broke out on the court and in the hallways leading to the gym." The paper quotes their coach, "We have it on film, girls. Hey, somebody call Sports Illustrated." In the locker room, we could dimly hear the commotion in the gym and the celebration in Perry's locker room as we sat quietly in a circle with Coach. Many players were crying. I mainly remember feeling numb. After we'd gathered ourselves a little, Coach Carter asked if we wanted to congratulate the other team, and we walked to Perry's locker room and shook their hands. Coach Carter is quoted in the Macon Telegraph, "We won like champs and we wanted to prove we could lose the same way."

I don't remember much about what happened right after that game, and my scrapbook has no notes, just articles from the newspapers covering our loss. Over the years, I've heard many stories about the sadness and shock that fans and teammates experienced. Our scorekeeper and manager Melodie Bohler was supposed to keep score for the boys' game that night, but she was crying so hard that the referee told her she couldn't sit at the scorers' table if she couldn't stop crying. She walked outside to try to calm herself, but even with the thirty minute delay as Perry celebrated, she couldn't keep the tears from falling, and somebody else had to keep the boys' book. Sandra Arnold told me recently that as we started toward the dressing room, somebody wrapped his arms around her. She was crying so hard she didn't even know who it was. It was not her boyfriend as she suspected, but her older brother Edward, who she had not realized was at the game. He wrote a letter to the Perry newspaper the next week (also published in the TC News), complimenting Perry's play but saying "Lady Vikings are still number 1!"

Many graduates and former Lady Vikings were in attendance at this game. Former player Jean Jones convinced her new boyfriend, Robert Cooper, to bring her to Perry from Middle Georgia College at Cochran. Her mother came to the game and met her boyfriend (who later became her husband) for the first time. Strangely enough, Robert only came to one other game, and it also turned out to be one that we lost. Another group, former player Dianne Kendrick, former manager Joyce Kendrick, and great fan Lynn Young, traveled from Georgia College. Mr. Cecil Kendrick, Diane's father, drove the 70 miles to Milledgeville to pick the girls up, drove them the 60 miles to Perry, and then drove them back to Milledgeville afterwards. They said it was a sad drive back to college. It was a sad drive home for the Lady Vikings as well. Years later, Shirley Durham said, "That drive from Perry was the longest I ever remember."

Coach had told us that we could come in late to school the next morning after the loss. When we arrived at 10 AM, our cheerleaders had plastered posters and signs all over the lobby, and students and teachers cheered for us as we walked through the hallways. In our English class, our teacher Mrs. Mickey Foreman read us inspirational quotes to help us deal with the loss. The most meaningful quote to me was from Charles Kettering, an inventor who said, "The only time you mustn't fail is the last time you try." I took that quote to heart and decided it was my theme for the rest of the season. It was my senior year, the last time I would try to win as a Lady Viking, and even though we'd lost a game, I knew we could still win the state championship.

Tommy Desselle wrote an article in the Macon Telegraph called "Streak Now History." The article quotes Coach Carter, "I think it was a miracle we won 132 consecutive contests. It's never been done before and I don't believe it'll ever be done again." While all the talk was about the end of our winning streak, our season wasn't over, and I wanted to keep the focus on the rest of the season. I wrote Mr. Desselle a letter thanking him for the article and telling him emphatically that we'd win the state championship in March.

We practiced the day after our loss, and Coach Carter told us,

"The pressure is off from the streak. We had a good ride and set a record that will be hard for anyone to beat. The season is not over, and our number one goal is still to win the state tournament." We had two important region games coming up that weekend, another on the next Tuesday night, and then the first game of the Tri-County Tournament the following weekend. We did not have time to dwell on the loss.

No. 33 Earline Flowers and No. 51 Shirley Durham wait for rebound in one of the contests against Haralson County.

After the Friday night game against Haralson County, the headline in the Columbus Enquirer read, "Lady Vikings Regain Touch." We won 58-54 and also won the next night in Carrollton. We continued winning games as we beat Talbotton on Tuesday night before heading to the Tri-County Tournament. Against Greenville in the first round, Mary Grover poured in six points in the second quarter and ended the game with 11 points, a career high for Mary, who rarely had played on the offensive end in her two seasons as a Lady Viking. In the final period of the Greenville game, the Rinky Dinks took the court. While our Rinky Dinks were usually awesome, Coach Carter got really mad at their play that night. Coach was alternating them on the court in the final quarter, and he called time-out. He told them they were not following instructions and had not scored a single goal nor played well on defense. He left the huddle, went to the official, and asked if he could have four on the court instead of six. The official said he could, so Coach returned to the huddle, called all the Rinky Dinks around him, and told them in no uncertain terms that he only saw four who wanted to play. He sent those four back out on the court and benched the rest. The game continued with those four playing both offense and defense. The coach of the other team got mad, thinking Coach Carter was trying to embarrass his team. Coach Carter immediately put six back in, and afterwards, he told the Rinky Dinks he wanted them to realize that it was important to follow his directions during every game, no matter the score. We won this first round game and would play the rest of the tournament the next weekend, with a game in Warner Robins in between.

My senior season was a tough one, both for the Lady Vikings and for my family. The day after the first round of the Tri-County Tournament, Mama got sick, and Daddy and I rushed her to the hospital. The small hospital in Butler was located in an old home, and the doctors were referred to as "Old Dr. Montgomery" and "Dr. Clifford," who was Old Dr. Montgomery's son. Dr. Clifford told Daddy that Mama needed surgery for an infection in her intestines. Dr. Clifford could do the surgery, but he'd need x-rays to guide him. There was a good x-ray machine in the larger town of Americus, so he asked Daddy and me to take Mama there for x-rays and bring them back to him. He'd perform the surgery on her in Butler the next day. Daddy and I set out for Americus with Mama lying in the back seat in tremendous pain. After we got the x-rays, the doctor in Americus told us that they needed to keep Mama and do the surgery there. He said he didn't believe she could make the forty-mile trip back to Butler. Daddy wavered and asked to call Dr. Clifford. Though the Americus doctor didn't seem to want to let Daddy make the call, he finally did. Dr. Clifford came on the line, and I could hear his booming voice talking to Daddy. "Bernard, they just want to do that surgery down there. You bring Lucibelle on back to Butler, and I'll get her fixed up. With the x-rays, I'll know what to do." The ride home was scary. Mama was hurting so badly, moaning whenever we'd go over the slightest bump. I held her hand from across the seat and worried and prayed all the way. The trip was hard on her, but we made it back to Butler, and Mama felt a little better once she was settled in the hospital bed. Dr. Clifford reassured her that he'd remove the infected areas of her intestine and she'd get better.

Dr. Clifford was known as a good surgeon, but skill wasn't all it took to perform surgery in a small hospital like ours. Dr. Clifford had a small plane, and when he performed surgery, he would fly the fifty miles to Columbus to pick up his surgery nurse. The morning of Mama's surgery, Daddy and I heard Dr. Clifford's plane coming in for a landing, and a few minutes later, his loud voice echoed through the hallways of the hospital as he and the nurse prepared for the surgery. People throughout Taylor County were praying for Mama, and those prayers were answered through the skilled hands of Dr. Clifford. Early that afternoon, a nurse came in to tell us that Dr. Clifford said the surgery was successful. Mama's recuperation would take a long time, but she'd get better. We were so relieved. As we sat there, Daddy said, "Well, you've got a game tonight, haven't you?" About that very time, Coach Carter stopped by the hospital where we were still waiting to see Mama. He said to me, "Now, you don't worry about playing this game at all. It's not a region game, so it doesn't affect our standings. There's no need for you to think you have to play." Daddy said he would leave it to me, that it might make me feel better to go to the game, and that Mama would be sleeping the entire time as she recovered from surgery. I told Coach I wanted to play.

Coach sent me in the car with his wife, and I will always appreciate how kind Mrs. Jane was to me that night on the ride to Warner Robins. She kept everything light and easy, first reassuring me that Mama would be all right, then telling funny stories about their children Cathy and Trey. Unfortunately, our second loss came that night. With the pressure off from the winning streak, Coach decided to try out some new strategies and treated the game as practice for the upcoming tournaments. I did not get the assignment of guarding Jeannie Mobley, their tall pivot player, like I had in Butler. Instead, Coach used Mary Riley in that position. Mary became frustrated, and at one point she slammed the ball on the floor when Mobley scored, drawing a technical foul. (After the game, Coach had Mary apologize to each of us for losing her temper.) We lost the game by one point, making it our second loss in two weeks, and it was disappointing to us to have a two in the loss column for the year's record so far (13-2). Up until a few weeks ago, I had never experienced a single loss as a Lady Viking, and now I had two. In my scrapbook, I pasted a picture from the Houston County newspaper of Perry Coach Bob Morrow and Warner Robins Coach Sid White captioned "Upset Masters," since they had both beaten the Lady Vikings. I wrote under it, "Get out the darts."

Life went on. Mama got better and left the hospital in a couple of weeks, weak but getting stronger. Dr. Clifford was proud that she pulled through that horrible infection, and when we went to Augusta later that spring to a specialist who did further surgeries, the doctor said Dr. Clifford's surgery had saved Mama's life. Mama didn't go to another game or teach school anymore that year, and she barely made it to my high school graduation, but she recuperated and returned to teaching the next fall. I come from strong stock. Daddy continued to attend my games, work, and keep us going at home. The year was hard, but we survived.

In the 1972 Tri-County tournament semi-final round against Yatesville, I remember being on the bench during the fourth quarter when a fan from the area said to Coach, "Norman, put Fuller back in and let her get 50 points. It's been a long time since we had a player score 50 in this gym." Coach just laughed and said, "We aren't interested in that." I ended the game with 47 points and didn't even play the whole game. The Manchester paper said, "Bunny Fuller, Taylor's irrepressible redhead, was her usual impressive self." We won the final round of the Tri-County Tournament against Harris County. The heat was not on in the gym and it was freezing, particularly for the fans, but not for Sandra Arnold, who had the hot hand that night. The Columbus Ledger Enquirer article by Roy Thomas says, "Miss Arnold scored 15 points, hitting on seven of nine floor shots from way out and adding a free throw." By today's rules, many of Sandra's shots would be three pointers. We had four players on the All-Tourney Team: Sandra Arnold, Shirley Durham, Earline Flowers, and me. The Manchester gym remained one of my favorite places to play.

We continued to play our regular season games with no more losses. Our last regular season game was against Marion County in Buena Vista. It was a great game for junior Carlyn Neisler, who scored ten points in the final three minutes. Carlyn just couldn't miss, and all of us on the bench cheered crazily with every shot. Even after our losses, the Lady Vikings still had spirit and camaraderie, and our season ended on a good note.

Then came our third and final loss of the year. We lost the finals of the sub-region tournament to Haralson County. Coach Carter had to spend the day in Atlanta at a State School Board Meeting, and he always says that he blames himself for that loss. Even though he left us in capable hands, he was not there for our pre-game rituals and just barely arrived from Atlanta for the beginning of the game. These rituals, including taping our ankles, giving a talk in the locker room, and saying a pre-game prayer, were an important part of our routine, and without them, our game was off. Haralson County was a good team and they were well-prepared to capitalize on our mistakes that night. Coach Carter told us in the locker room afterwards that if we had to lose a game in the tournaments, this was the one to lose because it didn't send us home; it meant that we'd play the sub-region champion the first night of region. We could still win region and state. He wiped tears from his eyes as he told us, "This loss is my fault. No matter what happens with my other job, the Lady Vikings are number one on my schedule, and I'll be with you every moment for the rest of the year." After Coach Carter left the locker room, we seniors called a players' meeting. We declared that losing was not fun, and that we were not going to do it again. If we did lose a game at this point in the tournaments, of course, it would be the worst "last" for the seniors: our last game of basketball as Lady Vikings. We wanted to play five more games. We wanted to win the semis and finals of region and three games in Macon at the State Class A Tournament.

Our next practice didn't start well. Before Coach Carter arrived, Shirley playfully challenged me to a one-on-one, saying she could block my shot. Never one to forego a competition, I said, "You know that's impossible!" and we went at it. Unfortunately, Shirley almost immediately sprained her ankle. We were helping her walk around the court to loosen up her ankle when word came that Coach's green Maverick was pulling up. Practice started, and Shirley was limping. "What happened?" Coach asked. Shirley said, "I was shooting a layup and came down wrong," with no mention of our one-on-one competition. I said nothing and prayed that the ankle would heal quickly. Shirley spent the next three days getting whirlpool treatments on the ankle and was finally able to practice on Thursday with her ankle taped. She was ready to play on Friday. Years later, Shirley still teases me about causing her to lie to Coach about how she hurt her ankle, and I still feel bad about that stupid one-on-one competition.

Qualifying for the state tournament was not an easy feat. We were in a region of Northwest Georgia schools and the region competition was held at Haralson County High School in Tallapoosa, 133 miles from Butler. We had to play Cartersville the first night, the all-important game determining if we would go to the state tourney. I remember looking at the printed program, and Taylor County was listed on the tourney bracket as the Region 4-A South Loser, a listing we had never seen before. We won that game handily over Cartersville and spent the night in Bremen at the Holiday Inn. We had an older fan named Mr. Hudson Poole who tried to attend all of our games. Mr. Hudson didn't drive after dark or far from home, and he called Coach Carter and sadly told him that he guessed he wouldn't be able to go to the region tournament games this year because he couldn't find a ride. Coach invited him to go along with the team and stay in the hotel room with him. Mr. Hudson was so excited. He'd just gotten out of the hospital, and he said "Dr. Whatley got me boosted up for the games!"

Our region finals opponent was Haralson County, the team that had just given us our third loss. The region game was our fourth meeting of the year and was on their home court in their new gym. After so many games, we were friends with the Haralson County team and their coach Jane Williamson. Sandra and I had met Coach Williamson at basketball camp the summer before, and she was well known throughout this section of the state for her short mini-skirts and her excellent girls basketball teams. Haralson County had some great players, including

Teresa Couch, Wanda Goldin, Clema Billingley, and the Goldin twins, Jo and Joy. Our player Carlyn Neisler says she remembers Coach giving her the assignment of "being" Teresa Couch in our practices. We had played them so many times during the two years they were in our region that Carlyn could mimic Couch's every move. I think they knew us just as well, and we knew the game to decide the region champion would be a good one. It was a hard fought contest, but we managed to win 44-41. The region 4-A title was ours. We plastered "On To Macon" on the locker room wall that Saturday night with used tape from our ankle wrappings. What we had worked so hard for was in our sights. I wrote in my scrapbook, "Player meeting is working so far." We would head to Macon for the state tournament the next week.

That Monday afternoon back at school, CBS news reporter Jed Duvall arrived to film a story about integration in our schools. Edie Smith and I were among the students Mr. Duvall interviewed. I told him that the successful basketball teams had given us all a common focus and helped the whole community come together. I never saw the segment, which aired nationally, but a top Georgia 4-H official told me later in the spring that he had seen it and that my comments had made his day. He was an older black gentleman whom I deeply respected, and I was proud that he praised my interview.

Our Thursday game in the quarter final round of the state tournament was scheduled at a strange time. We'd never played a game at 11 in the morning, and Coach was concerned that our usual fan base wouldn't be able to attend because of work. He knew we played better with our fans making noise in the cavernous Coliseum. As superintendent, he solved the problem by organizing a school-wide field trip to the game for anyone who wanted to go. Eleven buses drove Taylor County students to the Coliseum for our game. Coach said later that this game was the one time he felt like being superintendent and coach at the same time was advantageous. With so many excited fans there to cheer us on, we won easily over Central Gwinnett. When I came off the court after the game, I happened to see a little boy I knew from my summer work in Mama's classroom. He was sitting close to the court by himself eating his sack lunch. He looked up from his sandwich, recognized me, and said, "Did the Lady Vikings win?" I laughed, said yes, and escorted him back to his teacher. He obviously had no idea what was going on, but he was enjoying himself. Seeing and hearing all those kids in the stands of the Coliseum was amazing. Once again, Coach had controlled details that made such a difference.

Bunny Fuller looks at goal in the state tournament as Shirley Durham starts in for a pass.

The semi-final game saw us take on a familiar opponent: Miller County, who we'd played at state the year before. They had lost several starters to graduation, and our more experienced team beat them 66-44. Shirley, Sandra, and I scored in the double-figures. Meanwhile, Haralson County beat Bradwell Institute, and Coach Jane Williamson said her team was looking forward to the prospect of stopping Taylor's seniors in the next game.

With the championship on the line, we met Haralson County for the fifth time this season. The game was a hard-fought defensive contest. The worst moment of my basketball career occurred right before halftime when a Haralson County player accidentally elbowed Sandra Arnold in the mouth, knocking her front tooth all the way up into her gum. She had to leave the game, and I was so upset. The Fuller-Arnold combination on the basketball court could not end this way. With a few seconds left in the 2nd quarter, I heard over the loudspeaker, "Is there a dentist in the house? If so, please report to the locker rooms for Taylor County at the south end." In the meantime, Mr. Hubert Arnold had climbed the fence separating the fans from the court to check on his daughter. The managers had put an ice pack on her mouth, and they helped her to the locker room as the buzzer signaled halftime. Two dentists appeared from the crowd, and after a quick look, both said she should go to the emergency room. But when Coach Carter asked Sandra what she wanted to do, there was no hesitation on her part. "It's my last game. I want to play." After halftime and some aspirin, Sandra returned to the game to wild cheering from our fans. The Haralson fans cheered for her as well. I breathed a sigh of relief when she was once again on the floor in the third quarter with an incredible show of courage. The Fuller-Arnold combination wasn't over for two more seven minute quarters. The score went back and forth the entire third and fourth quarter until we pulled ahead to win the game 51-45 and take the title.

Accompanied by a slew of fans holding up five fingers and yelling "Five in a Row!", we accepted our fifth state championship trophy for the Taylor County High School Lady Vikings. We seniors had succeeded in making our "last" game as we wanted it to be. I remembered the quote from Mrs. Foreman's class: "The only time you mustn't fail is the last time you try."

I had never known if reporter Tommy Deselle got the letter I wrote him after our loss to Perry, telling him that we would win the state tournament. After the state championship, he wrote that even after our winning streak ended, "Bunny Fuller, who Carter calls 'the best pivot player in the state,' predicted another state crown," so I knew that he had. The next day, the all-tournament teams were published in the Macon Telegraph, and I received the Most Valuable Player award. Sandra Arnold, Shirley Durham, Mary Grover, and I were named to the all-state team. Later that spring, Sandra Arnold, Shirley Durham, and I received the honor of having our uniforms retired.

After all the challenges we had faced, all the controversy from integration, all the pride and pressure of the winning streak, all the disappointment when we lost our first game, we had prevailed. When a team wins the state championship, their season never ends. They don't have to look back and wonder "What if?" because they've gotten the ultimate prize, the claim to the best in their league.

Coach Carter takes the mic to accept the 1972 state championship with Bunny Fuller, Sandra Arnold, and Edie Smith.

In the dressing room after the trophy presentation, the team, cheerleaders, and managers celebrate the fifth state championship by the Lady Vikings.

There Was Once a Team

As we players discovered in our years as Lady Vikings, life goes on. The 1972 season, my senior year, was Norman Carter's last season as a coach. His overall record over twelve years of coaching was 350-32 for a state record .916 winning percentage. He continued his Norman Carter Basketball School for Girls for 25 years, improving the basketball skills of over 10,000 girls from across the state. In 1996, he and his wife Mrs. Jane founded The Golden Rule, a rehabilitation facility for women who abuse drugs and alcohol. More than 1,500 women so far have benefitted from The Golden Rule, located in the Taylor County community of Mauk. He served as superintendent in Taylor County for 21 years and then continued work in public education on a state and regional level, most recently as director of the Chattahoochee-Flint Regional Education Service Agency.

Life went on for all the players as well. After graduation, I attended Middle Georgia College in Cochran for two years and then finished my education degree at the University of Georgia. I played basketball at both schools and was Scholar Athlete of the Year for 1976 at UGA. Years later, an alumni association erected a monument behind Stegman Coliseum honoring UGA athletes, and my name appears on it along with football star Herschel Walker, Olympian Teresa Edwards, and other UGA athletes. I returned to Taylor County to teach, and a few years later I married Mark Harris, another former basketball standout who played on a state championship team led by Coach Carter. We had a daughter, and our lives were busy with raising her, working, and enjoying our family and friends.

A few times a year, our family would get together at Mr. Frank and Mrs. Sarah Riley's house. Like me, Judy and Sissy were married with families of their own. At these parties, the talk would always turn to basketball and the winning streak years. Judy, Sissy, and I loved to reminisce about how much we'd learned and how much fun we'd had as Lady Vikings. As the years went by, we wondered sometimes if our streak would be broken, if another team in Georgia would win more consecutive games than our 132 in a row record. It hasn't happened yet.

Finally, Judy, Sissy and I decided that it was time for a team reunion. We held the reunion in March of 2007, when we players were in our fifties and Coach Carter in his sixties. As we made plans, many of our families, friends, and co-workers got involved to help, and a whirlwind of activity began as everyone focused once again on those magical winning streak years. Judy's daughter Beth said, "This re-union has taken on a life of its own!" I started a blog where players, managers, fans, and cheerleaders posted their memories. My daughter Katie, then a teacher at Taylor County Middle School, worked with a student group to create a movie about the winning streak for a competition on unsung Georgia heroes. A news station from Macon, Channel 13 WMAZ, sent a reporter over to Butler to log a story on the reunion. We all figured the story would be short, but it seems Coach Carter worked his famous charm and charisma on the reporter during his interview, because the story ended up being four minutes long. In speaking about how difficult it was to win 132 games in a row, Coach Carter said, "Some say it was easy to do back then. Well, if it was so easy to do, why didn't somebody else do it?"

We held the reunion in the Taylor County Elementary School lunchroom, the only venue in the county equipped for a catered meal and celebration for a large crowd. Thirty-five years after the 1972 State Championship, about 200 Lady Vikings gathered to remember the great days and stand in awe of the fact that we'd set a state record that might never be broken. The school lunchroom was transformed with navy blue and silver flags hanging from the ceiling. The state trophies were displayed on the stage, and huge posters of the teams and action shots from games lined the walls. We also displayed memorabilia from the winning streak years, including uniforms, Sandra Arnold's lucky kneepad, championship rings, and players' scrapbooks. Three screens around the room played a slideshow of pictures and movies for all the crowd to see. Coach's family of Mrs. Jane, Cathy, Trey and wife Beth, as well as the grandchildren attended. One grandchild said, "I didn't know Granddaddy was famous!" The day after the reunion, Coach Carter wrote on the blog about how much the reunion meant to him: "Next to my marriage and the birth of my children and grandchildren, this will be my most memorable event."

When we started planning the reunion, we also set in motion a campaign to get Coach Carter and the Lady Vikings more state recognition for the winning streak. Several things happened at the reunion to call us to action. During the program, we showed the movie my daughter and her students had made, and many attendees were shocked when they learned from the movie that there was no mention of Coach Carter or the Lady Vikings in the Georgia Sports Hall of Fame. Ed Grisamore, a columnist for the Macon Telegraph, was a featured speaker at the reunion, and he said he would do everything in his power to help Coach Carter and the teams be recognized in the Hall.

After the reunion, our push to get Coach Carter inducted into the Hall of Fame began in earnest. Judy and I updated Coach Carter's application, and the Hall of Fame was inundated with emails from his players, fans, and friends. Ed Grisamore wrote an article about Coach Carter, subtly questioning why he'd never been inducted in the Hall of Fame. The article says, "By now, the Georgia Sports Hall of Fame is very familiar with Carter. Ever since the Lady Vikings teams held their 35-year reunion in late March, folks from Butler, Reynolds, Potterville and points between have been waging a full-court press to have their coach immortalized." In late summer of 2007, the Georgia Sports Hall of Fame announced that it would induct Coach Norman Carter as part of the Class of 2008. Of course, a large crowd came to support Coach Carter at the induction ceremony. At one point during the ceremony, emcee Ron Jaworski turned toward the Carters at the head table and asked in awe, "One hundred thirty-two in a row?" He repeated the question twice more until Coach finally answered with a smile, "Yes!" The crowd from Taylor County cheered the longest and the loudest, just as we had at our long-ago basketball games!

The next spring, the Georgia Sports Hall of Fame Museum unveiled an exhibit about the Lady Vikings' winning streak. The exhibit featured some of the memorabilia we had displayed at the reunion, including letterman jackets, team pictures, and retired uniforms. The exhibit also had a description of the winning streak and the five championships we had won.

Over the years, the Lady Vikings have continued to be featured in newspaper articles and tv news stories about the streak. In 2008, Atlanta Journal columnist Jeff Haws and other sports writers compiled a list of the greatest dynasties in Georgia High School sports. The Lady Vikings made the top ten, coming in at number six. The article says, "While they were winning five consecutive state titles and a state-record [132] consecutive games (tied for [fourth]-best all-time nationally), they also found time to play a key role in integrating sports in the state." That same year, Sandra Arnold, Judy Riley Bland, Sissy Riley Martin, and I, along with Coach Carter, had our picture on the front page of the Atlanta Journal sports section in an article by Todd Holcomb titled "Remember the Vikings" about the winning streak. In 2012, the Macon Telegraph ran a special series called "The Numbers Game." Over the course of several months, the weekly series named an outstanding athlete from the Middle Georgia area for each jersey number 1-99, and I was chosen for number 35. I didn't know I was featured until a friend shared the article on Facebook, and I had no idea of some of the statistics it includes about me. According to the article by Jonathan Heeter:

> "Fuller's teams went 117-3 during her four years, never lost in Taylor County and won state championships all four seasons. Fuller averaged around 22 points for her career. She scored more than 2,200 points in high school, finishing with at least 23 30-point games and four 40-point games with a career high of 47. Her best season came as a sophomore in 1969-70 when she averaged 29.4 points... Stats for 22 of her high school games, including 10 during her senior year, are missing, so you can only guess what that does to her already impressive high school stats."

Coach Carter always emphasized teamwork over individual accomplishments, but it made me proud to read about how I had helped the Lady Vikings achieve success.

Coach Carter's achievements also continue to receive recognition and honors. On October 9, 2015, the high school gym in Taylor County was named the Carter-Troutman Gymnasium, in honor of two of the best girls basketball coaches in the state: Norman Carter and Matt Troutman. (Matt's wife is former Lady Viking Shirley Durham.) I got to speak on my favorite subject, Coach Norman Carter, in the naming ceremony, and many former players and families were in attendance. As I walked to the lectern to give my speech, Coach gave me that smile and wink that I knew so well and that always filled me with confidence.

When Coach retired in 2016 after 57 years in public education, many educators, friends, family, and former basketball players attended his retirement party. In his speech, he said, “People have often asked why I’m so terse. A basketball timeout is only a minute. I’d tell my players to run over to the huddle, look me right in the eye, and listen. You can get a lot said in one minute... I think I’m a pretty good judge of basketball-playing ability, but I’m an even better judge of character, and that’s how we did so well.” I’ve always believed that much of Coach’s success came from his ability to analyze a situation and make a decision quickly. His calm certainty gave his players and employees confidence, both in him and in themselves.

When I look back at my scrapbooks now, I wonder if the winning streak will ever be beaten. I don’t think so. As the editor of the Taylor County News wrote in an article I saved, “Future generations...may find it hard to believe that there was once a team…” Once.

L to R: Judy Riley Bland, Sandra Arnold, Coach Norman Carter, Bunny Fuller Harris, Sissy Riley Martin.

L to R: Sandra Arnold, Judy Riley Bland, Coach Norman Carter, Bunny Fuller Harris, Sissy Riley Martin.

Lady Vikings Lessons and Memories

The following are quotes from Lady Vikings players and fans.

From the Taylor County student-created movie "132-0":

The town would empty. And you'd have people over there [at the state tournament] who you didn't even think liked basketball.

-Frank Riley, Lady Vikings parent

The biggest reason for our success in all these state tournaments was that nobody cared who got the credit for winning. It was a total team effort.

-Sissy Riley Martin, Lady Viking

It wasn't just one person that played on the Vikings. It wasn't just the starting players. It was all the players, it was the bench, it was the cheerleaders, it was the scorekeepers, the fans, everybody, the whole county.

-Sandra Arnold, Lady Viking

We pulled together as people, as human beings working toward a goal.

-Shirley Durham Troutman, Lady Viking

Playing [against] them was an honor for us, just to be on the floor with them at that time, because they were that good.

-Amy Denson Hardman,
Lady Vikings opponent from Harris County

They'll always be heroes in the hearts of everyone in Taylor County.

-Buddy Dunn, Lady Vikings fan

From reunion video "Magic":

Coach made each and every one of us feel like we were a vital part of the team.

-Karon Peed Dunn, Lady Viking

From "Lady Vikings Winning Streak Years" blog:

*In spite of my complete fear of disappointing Coach Carter, I too have many life lessons learned from the basketball experience: when faced with a setback, keep your eye on the bigger picture (definitely learned the night of THE loss); it takes a team to win; fundamentals, planning, practice and hard work are the keys to success; win with class and face defeat the same way; always anticipate. When I see other successful teams, whether in sports or other activities, these characteristics are usually present. I am thankful that I had the opportunity to learn these lessons while having fun playing basketba*ll.

-Harriet Jones Geesey, Lady Viking

We won the tournament, of course. I don't mean to sound cocky but we always won. Don't misunderstand; the Lady Vikings didn't take their skills for granted. Every game was a contest in its own right. Every game was exciting. Every game my voice was added to the roar of the crowd. I'm proud to say that I was a Viking manager during the Lady Viking's 132 game winning streak and I was a part of the phenomenon.

-Melodie Bohler Stinson, Lady Vikings manager

Coach Carter taught us all that it takes hard work to be successful. That is true in basketball but also true in life. It was anything but easy playing for Coach Carter. We all remember coming back to the gym in Butler to practice late at night after a bad game and him daring us to shiver in that very cold gym. We were all afraid of him but we also had great respect for him. But despite his toughness we all knew he cared about us as individuals. The day my dad died my junior year was obviously a very traumatic time in my life. I remember the crowd of people at our house that night and I remember looking up and seeing Coach Carter walking down the hall. I can count the true heroes in my life on one hand. Coach Carter is in that group. The lessons I learned with all the girls who were part of the mighty Taylor County Lady Vikings are the greatest lessons I ever learned in life. I thank God for allowing me to be a part of that team and to get to experience what we experienced.

-Kathy Underwood Goddard, Lady Viking

The momentum of what Norman Carter had done with basketball was felt throughout Middle Georgia. He had become a legend and had earned the respect of his players and colleagues alike. I often think back and wonder what it was. He created in us an absolute love for the sport. If you were not totally committed 100% to basketball and the program, then there was no place for you. Coach Carter demanded respect and raised the bar for all of us to achieve the very best in all areas of our lives. What people fail to understand was that he made us better people for it. We were expected to be academically high achievers. We held our heads high wherever we went. We were proud of who we were, because we knew that we had been set apart.

-Carol Dyar, Lady Viking

I don't think it ever occurred to any of us as members of the Lady Vikings basketball teams to want any glory for ourselves as individual players. We wouldn't have dared! Our streak was a prime example of teamwork and what the results can be if everyone pulls together and keeps their eyes on the task at hand. I think the fans from our team and others noticed it about us as well. It was also a result of what Coach Carter learned about coaching a bunch of girls along the way! These years taught us all a lot about teamwork which has paid off for me in my career. It did not matter who got the credit or made the points. We just wanted someone to!

-Judy Riley Bland, Lady Viking

Coach Carter brought out the best in us and in the process we received confidence in ourselves and respect for others that we carried beyond the court. I get to see Coach Carter from time to time when he brings his Golden Rule girls to our church. From the choir as I see him in the crowd I stand a little taller and I sing a little louder. I guess I'm still trying to impress him to "Put me in, Coach, I'm ready to play!"

-Susan Whidden Cox Corpus, Lady Viking

Playing basketball for Norman Carter was an awesome experience. We all had the great desire to please him each time we hit the hardwoods. He had the ability to motivate us all to do our best.

-Kathy Peed Davis, Lady Viking

When I think about the girls on these teams, I remember that people would be surprised when we came in that we were not huge, rough looking tomboys. We were just well coached and totally focused on the job at hand

-Sissy Riley Martin, Lady Viking

From Facebook:

The most special group of people I've ever been involved with was the Taylor County Lady Vikings. When I joined the team as a freshman, I was apprehensive that I would be seen as an intruder since I came from Reynolds, and unlike Bunny and Sandra, was not overly blessed with talent, but I never felt anything but welcome. I think there was an absence of ego with that group that I cannot begin to explain, but I think it played a big part in the winning streak. The trite saying "There's no 'me' in team" doesn't begin to express the sublimity of actually having an experience where everyone, from the superstars to the bottom of the bench, put the good of the team ahead of anyone's personal ambition.

-Jean Jones Cooper, Lady Viking

	1966-67 TC Lady Vikings	Won Consolation Game to begin the Winning Streak	
	Name	Uniform No.	Grade
1	Linda Hill	10	12
2	Diane Wall	11	10
3	JoAnne Parks	12	9
4	Karon Peed	12	9
5	Grace Bussey	13	11
6	Linda Joiner	14	10
7	Sissy Riley	15	10
8	Patty Singleton	22	12
9	Vicki Harris	23	12
10	Maxine Lawhorn	24	10
11	Sue Lawhorn	25	11
12	Lynne Partain	32	10
13	Gail Woodall	32	10
14	Joye McCrary	33	12
15	Kathy Peed	33	9
16	Judy Riley	34	9
17	Donna Minor	44	10

18	Jean Burke	Shared uniform	9
19	Donna Pittman	Shared uniform	9
20	Denease McAbee	Shared uniform	9
21	Glenda Gassett	Shared uniform	9
	Martha Clark, Bucky Reddish, Roger Smith	Managers	
	Karen Parks, Charlene Wright, Corine Parks, Glenda Mullins, Margie Wainwright, Paula Lee	Cheerleaders	

	1967-68 TC Lady Vikings	Won Games 2-63 of the Winning Streak	Record 31-0
	Name	Uniform No.	Grade
1	Patsy Ranow	10	9
2	Diane Wall	11	11
3	Denease McAbee	12	10
4	Grace Bussey	13	12
5	Linda Joiner	14	11
6	Sissy Riley	15	11
7	Kathy Peed	21	10
8	Maxine Lawhorn	23	11

9	Sue Lawhorn	25	12
10	Karon Peed	30	10
11	Judy Riley	34	10
12	Donna Minor	44	12
13	Regina Parks	Shared uniform	9
14	Marianne Hinton	Shared uniform	9
15	Dianne Kendrick	Shared uniform	9
16	Sharon Barfield	Shared uniform	9
17	Sandra Guined	Shared uniform	9
	Beth Jones, Priscilla Jones, Laroy Barrow, Gary Payne	Managers	
	Paula Lee, Karen Parks, Margie Wainwright, Charlene Wright, Judy Scott, Linda Blackston, JoAnn Parks	Cheerleaders	

	1968-69 TC Lady Vikings	Won Games 33-63 of the Winning Streak	Record 31-0
	Name	Uniform No.	Grade
1	Patsy Ranow	10	10

2	Diane Wall	11	12
3	Debra Spillers	12	9
4	Maxine Lawhorn	13	12
5	Linda Joiner	14	12
6	Sissy Riley	15	12
7	Jean Jones	20	9
8	Kathy Peed	21	11
9	Sandra Guined	22	10
10	Betty Williams	23	9
11	Beth Barrow	24	9
12	Regina Parks	25	10
13	Karon Peed	30	11
14	Sandra Arnold	31	9
15	Dianne Kendrick	32	10
16	Marianne Hinton	33	10
17	Judy Riley	34	11
18	Bunny Fuller	35	9
19	Denease McAbee	44	11

	Beth Jones, Priscilla Jones, Laroy Barrow, Gary Payne, Joyce Kendrick, Melodie Bohler, Roger Smith	Managers
	May Parks, Jean Burke, Sharon Barfield, Charlene Albritton, Linda Blackston, Charlene Wright, Judy Scott, Karen Parks	Cheerleaders

	1969-70 TC Lady Vikings	Won Games 64-94 of the Winning Streak	Record 31-0	
	Name	Uniform No.	Height	Grade
	Freshmen shared uniforms, so some numbers are the same.			
1	Patsy Ranow	10	5’6”	11
2	Edie Smith	11	5’4’	9
3	Jan Hobbs	11	5’4”	9
4	Carlyn Neisler	13	5’7”	9
5	Carol Wall	13	5’6”	9
6	Kathy Underwood	14	5’5”	9
7	Kathy Peed	20	5’7”	12
8	Jean Jones	21	5’5”	10

9	Sandra Guined	22	5'4"	11
10	Betty Williams	23	5'4"	10
11	Cecilia Kendrick	24	5'4"	9
12	Mary Jane Robinson	24	5'6"	9
13	Regina Parks	25	5'7"	11
14	Karon Peed	30	5'9"	12
15	Sandra Arnold	31	5'5"	10
16	Dianne Kendrick	32	5'8"	11
17	Marianne Hinton	33	5'6"	11
18	Judy Riley	34	5'10"	12
19	Bunny Fuller	35	5'10"	10
20	Denease McAbee	44	5'7"	9
	Beth Jones, Laroy Barrow, Joyce Kendrick, Buster Hobbs, Melodie Bohler, Gary Payne, Roger Smith	Managers		
	Sharon Barfield, Charlene Albritton, Gail Braddy, May Parks, Carlene Hobbs, Julie Hogan, Dawn Pennington	Cheerleaders		

	1970-71 TC Lady Vikings	Won Games 95-124 of the Winning Streak	Record 30-0	
	Name	Uniform No.	Height	Grade
1	Patsy Ranow	10	5'6"	12
2	Edie Smith	11	5'6"	10
3	Carlyn Neisler	12	5'8"	10
4	Carol Dyar	13	5'8"	10
5	Mary Riley	14	5'7"	11
6	Jean Jones	20	5'5"	11
7	Mary Grover	21	5'5"	11
8	Harriet Jones	22	5'6"	9
9	Faye Hayes	23	5'5"	10
10	Susan Whidden	24	5'4"	9
11	Regina Parks	25	5'8"	12
12	Cecilia Kendrick	30	5'4"	10
13	Sandra Arnold	31	5'5"	11
14	Dianne Kendrick	32	5'7"	12
15	Earline Flowers	33	5'5"	11
16	Bunny Fuller	35	5'10"	11

17	Kathy Underwood	44	5'5"	10
18	Shirley Durham	54	5'6'	11
	Joyce Kendrick, Melodie Bohler, Gary Payne, Buster Hobbs, Wayne Smith, Calvin Coleman, Jimmy Harbuck, Bill James	Managers		
	Dawn Pennington, Charlene Carter, Sherry Parks, Debbie Johnson, Julie Hogan	Cheerleaders		

	1971-72 TC Lady Vikings	Won Games 125-132 of the Winning Streak		
	Name	Uniform No.	Height	Grade
1	Carlyn Neisler	12	5'8"	11
2	Cynthia Carter	13	5'2"	10
3	Mary Riley	14	5'7"	12
4	Mary Grover	21	5'4"	12
5	Harriet Jones	22	5'6"	10
6	Susan Whidden	24	5'6"	10
7	Kathy Underwood	25	5'4"	11

8	Edie Smith	30	5’4”	11
9	Sandra Arnold	31	5’4”	12
10	Vicki Works	32	5’2”	10
11	Earline Flowers	33	5’4”	12
12	Bunny Fuller	35	5’10”	12
13	Carol Dyar	44	5’7”	11
14	Shirley Durham	51	5’4”	12
15	Amy Sherten	Shared	5'5"	9
16	Sharon Kendrick	Shared	5’8”	9
17	Kathy Townes	Shared	5’5”	9
18	Sharon Johnson	Shared	5’6”	9
19	Teresa Parks	Shared	5'8"	9
20	Nancy Bone	Shared	5’5”	9
	Melodie Bohler, Faye Hayes, Robbin Works	Managers		
	Debbie Johnson, Sherry Parks, Jeannette Dent, Angela Peed, Julie Hogan Mary Jane Robinson, Dawn Pennington	Cheerleaders		

132 Games Without a Loss by the Taylor County Lady Vikings

Year	Game No.	Location	Score
1967	1	Pike County Region Consolation Game	W
1967-68	2	at Crawford County	W
	3	Pike County	W
	4	at Talbot County	W
	5	at Marion County	57-42
	6	Harris County	49-44
	7	Marion County	W
	8	Crawford County	51-24
	9	at Harris County	W
	10	Macon County	W
	11	at Perry	W
	12	at Mary Persons	W
	13	Tri-County Tourney vs E. Coweta	W
	14	Tri-County Tourney vs Greenville	52-37
	15	Tri-County Tourney vs Harris County	38-29
	16	at Fort Valley	46-37
	17	R.E. Lee	62-44
	18	Talbot County	W
	19	Mary Persons	78-52
	20	Perry	W
	21	at Pike County	W
	22	at R.E. Lee	W

132 Games Without a Loss
by the Taylor County Lady Vikings

	23	at Macon County	W
	24	Fort Valley	W
	25	Sub-Region at Barnesville vs Jackson	W
	26	Sub-Region at Barnesville vs Pike County	53-46
	27	Region at Villa Rica vs Hogansville	51-35
	28	Region at Villa Rica vs Valley Point	55-37
	29	Region at Villa Rica vs Harris County	56-22
	30	State Tourney at Macon City Auditorium vs Stone Mountain	71-54
	31	State Tourney at Macon City Auditorium vs Telfair County	51-37
	32	State Tourney at Macon City Auditorium vs Harris County	41-24
1968-69	33	Crawford County	72-32
	34	Talbot County	57-17
	35	Flint River Academy	88-38
	36	at Marion County	66-28
	37	Yatesville	58-26
	38	Perry	60-38
	39	at Crawford County	62-43
	40	at Flint River Academy	71-45
	41	at Perry	70-51
	42	Northside	59-37
	43	Americus	48-26
	44	Marion County	63-32
	45	at Mary Persons	75-35

132 Games Without a Loss by the Taylor County Lady Vikings

	46	at Talbot County	49-16
	47	Mary Persons	70-40
	48	at Yatesville	W
	49	Tri-County Tourney vs Western	66-26
	50	Tri-County Tourney vs Yatesville	61-33
	51	Tri-County Tourney vs Greenville	63-53
	52	at Northside	51-34
	53	at Americus	W
	54	at Harris County	55-29
	55	Harris County	W
	56	Sub Region at Thomaston vs Yatesville	48-26
	57	Sub-Region at Thomaston vs Crawford County	52-26
	58	Region at Talbotton vs Pike County	47-33
	59	Region at Talbotton vs Milner	56-39
	60	State Tourney at Talbotton vs Toombs Central	46-25
	61	State Tourney at Macon Coliseum vs Doerun	63-29
	62	State Tourney at Macon Coliseum vs Glascock County	61-53
	63	State Tourney at Macon Coliseum vs Cave Spring	36-32
1969-70	64	at Talbot County	67-30
	65	Flint River Academy	73-48
	66	Marion County	79-32
	67	at Crawford County	84-22
	68	at Yatesville	76-36

132 Games Without a Loss by the Taylor County Lady Vikings

	69	Perry	63-39
	70	Harris County	73-38
	71	Crawford County	69-37
	72	at Americus	71-42
	73	at Perry	58-41
	74	at Milner	W
	75	at Marion County	68-29
	76	Mary Persons	W
	77	at Flint River Acad.	W
	78	Talbot County	63-30
	79	Yatesville	45-30
	80	Tri-County Tourney vs Western	85-20
	81	at Mary Persons	W
	82	Tri-County Tourney vs Harris County	73-46
	83	Tri-County Tourney vs Yatesville	66-42
	84	Americus	70-61
	85	Milner	56-26
	86	at Harris County	47-17
	87	Sub-Region at Thomaston vs Crawford County	63-43
	88	Sub-Region at Thomaston vs Yatesville	59-35
	89	Region at Thomaston vs Greenville	60-56
	90	Region at Thomaston vs Pike County	74-59
	91	State Tourney at Fairburn vs Temple	54-38
	92	State Tourney at Macon Coliseum vs Laurens County	53-26

132 Games Without a Loss by the Taylor County Lady Vikings

	93	State Tourney at Macon Coliseum vs Norman Park	52-49
	94	State Tourney at Macon Coliseum vs Stratford	68-50
1970-71	95	at Marion County	71-44
	96	Crawford County	99-37
	97	at Pike County	57-33
	98	at Crawford County	69-43
	99	at Mary Persons	W
	100	Manchester	65-33
	101	at Fayette County	63-30
	102	at Perry	40-38
	103	at Manchester	60-35
	104	Marion County	63-43
	105	Mary Persons	81-38
	106	at Villa Rica	56-36
	107	Pike County	58-33
	108	Tri-County Tourney vs Yatesville	56-29
	109	at Warner Robins	47-45 2 OTs
	110	Tri-County Tourney vs Harris County	62-30
	111	Tri-County Tourney vs Manchester	63-40
	112	Warner Robins	55-42
	113	Villa Rica	60-15
	114	Haralson County	W
	115	Carrolton	58-34
	116	Perry	70-60

132 Games Without a Loss by the Taylor County Lady Vikings

	117	at Fayette County	W
	118	Sub-Region at Fayette County vs Haralson County	55-53
	119	Region at Rockmart vs Model	53-29
	120	Region at Rockmart vs Cartersville	57-54
	121	State Tourney at Macon Coliseum vs Vidalia	57-40
	122	State Tourney at Macon Coliseum vs Putnam County	44-22
	123	State Tourney at Macon Coliseum vs Miller County	53-37
	124	State Tourney at Macon Coliseum vs Berkmar	49-43
1971-72	125	Marion County	65-43
	126	at Crawford County	58-30
	127	Warner Robins	67-63
	128	at Crawford County	77-40
	129	at Manchester	W
	130	Perry	56-51
	131	at Fayette County	W
	132	Talbot County	71-45
		at Perry (1st loss since 1967)	48-53
		State Tourney vs Central Gwinnett	48-42
		State Tourney vs Miller Co.	66-44
		State Tourney vs Haralson Co.	51-45

1966-67 Lady Vikings. Having won twenty-two games in a row during the season, this team lost in the semi-finals of the sub-region. The team then won the consolation game of the tournament. This was the first game of the 132 game winning streak.

The 1967-68 Taylor County Lady Vikings had a 31-0 record for the season and won games 2-32 of the sinning streak.

- *All-State 1968: Grace Bussey, Linda Joiner, Sue Lawhorn, Sissy Riley, Diane Wall*
- *Most Valuable Forward in State Tournament 1968: Sissy Riley*

The 1968-69 Taylor County Lady Vikings had a 31-0 record for the season and won games 33-63 of the winning streak.

- *All-State 1969: Linda Joiner, Sissy Riley, Denease McAbee, Diane Wall*
- *Most Valuable Forward in State Tournament 1969*
- *Uniform Retired: Sissy Riley*

The 1969-70 Taylor County Lady Vikings had a 31-0 record for the season and won games 64-94 of the winning streak.

- *All-State 1970: Judy Riley, Bunny Fuller, Karon Peed, Kathy Peed, Denease McAbee*
- *Most Valuable Forward in State Tournament 1970: Bunny Fuller*

The 1970-71 Taylor County Lady Vikings had a 30-0 record for the season and won games 95-124 of the winning streak.

- *All State 1971: Patsy Ranow, Regina Parks, Sandra Arnold, Shirley Durham, Bunny Fuller*
- *Most Valuable Forward 1971 State Tournament: Bunny Fuller*
- *Most Valuable Guard 1971 State Tourament: Patsy Ranow*

The 1971-72 Taylor County Lady Vikings won the first eight games of the season – games 125-132 of the winning streak. The team lost three games during the season, but in March they won the 1972 Class A State Championship.

- *All-State 1972: Sandra Arnold, Shirley Durham, Mary Grover, Bunny Fuller*
- *Most Valuable Player in State Tournament 1972: Bunny Fuller*
- *Uniforms Retired: Sandra Arnold, Shirley Durham, Bunny Fuller*

Bunny Fuller Harris